At Home in
South Carolina

At Home in South Carolina

Suzanne H. McDaniel
Sandra G. Thomas
Thomas R. McDaniel

SANDLAPPER
PUBLISHING, INC.

Orangeburg, South Carolina

At Home in South Carolina

Design and Production by:
Faith Nance and Eleanor Cameron
Illustrations by:
Darby Erd and Robin M.N. Richards
Cover design by:
Robin M.N. Richards

Library of Congress Cataloging-in Publication Data

McDaniel, Suzanne H., 1942-
    At home in South Carolina / Suzanne H. McDaniel, Sandra G.Thomas, Thomas R. McDaniel.
       p.   cm.
    Includes index.
    Summary: Describes the history and geography of South Carolina for third graders.
    ISBN 0-87844-099-2 : $18.17
    1. South Carolina–History–Juvenile literature. 2. South Carolina–Geography–Juvenile literature. [1. South Carolina.]
I. Thomas, Sandra G., 1946- . II. McDaniel, Thomas R. , 1941
III. Title.
F269.M37 1991
975.7–dc20   91-13873
                                    CIP
                                    AC

We dedicate this book to our children–Robb and Katy McDaniel, Beth and Katie Thomas–and to all of the children who want to learn about their home in South Carolina.

About the Authors

SUZANNE H. MCDANIEL is Social Studies Coordinator and coordinator of Programs for the Gifted in Spartanburg School District No. 7. She has over twenty-five years of experience as a teacher, administrator, and writer of instructional materials.

SANDRA G. THOMAS is Chief Supervisor for Resource Development, Office of Instructional Technology, South Carolina Department of Education. She has been working on studies of South Carolina for eighteen years.

THOMAS R. MCDANIEL is Vice President for Academic Affairs and Dean of the College at Converse College. He has over twenty-five years experience as a teacher and professor and over 100 publications in education and humanities.

CONTENTS

Preface

At Home in South Carolina is a comprehensive social studies text. Its special focus is the geography, culture, and heritage of our home state, but the authors have incorporated in the instructional program all of the important concepts and skills of history and the social studies found in most basal third grade social studies texts. We believe it is not only possible but *desirable* to teach history, government, economics, anthropology, and (even) environmental studies within a text on South Carolina. We have also given you a text that incorporates basic skills (keyed to BSAP objectives), higher order thinking skills, reading and listening skills, map and globe skills, research and reference skills, and cooperative learning skills. We believe the special features–like "Read-To-Me" and "A Closer Look"–will help keep students interested and involved in learning about social studies *and* South Carolina. This is, after all, a book for and about them.

As you look at the text (and the instructional strategies, activities, reviews, and resources in the teacher's guide), think about the value of combining a study of our state with the general goals of social studies instruction. We believe you will find that this comprehensive approach will provide you the coverage and the flexibility that you and your students want. Best wishes for an exciting study of South Carolina.

INTRODUCTION

This is a book about you. It is about the place you live. It is about the people who live near you. It is about your family, your community, your state. It is also about people who lived here before you.

You are a South Carolinian. You live in the state of South Carolina. This book tells the story of your home state. It tells what it means to be a South Carolinian.

Geography

In this book you will study the place where you live. This study is called **geography.** You will find out where your state is. You will learn where places are in your state.

You will learn about the land and water here. You will find out how important our land and water are. And you will learn ways to keep our land and water beautiful and useful.

You will learn about our plants and animals. You will learn how we protect them.

Culture

In this book you will also study how we South Carolinians live. How we live is called our **culture.**

You will learn about kinds of work South Carolinians do.

You will learn what we do for fun.

You will talk about things we like to eat. You will see how we dress.

These things are all part of our culture.

Heritage

In this book you will study things that have happened in our state. This study is called **history.** You will find out how people lived here long ago. You will see how things have changed in our state.

You will learn about things earlier South Carolinians did. You will learn what they have passed on to us. The things they have passed on are our **heritage.**

We, the writers, have three hopes for you as you read this book. We hope you will learn that South Carolina is more than a place on a map. We hope you will learn what it means to be a South Carolinian. And we hope you will love your home in South Carolina as much as we do.

YOUR HOME STATE

Do you know where your home is? Perhaps you know your address. Does it look something like this?

Is South Carolina part of your address, too? If it is, you are a South Carolinian. South Carolina is your home.

But where is South Carolina? And what is it? That is what this unit is all about.

UNIT 1

CHAPTER

1
Locating South Carolina

2
Locating Your Home

In this unit, you will learn that:

1. South Carolina is an area on the earth.
2. South Carolina has a special shape.
3. Our state is part of a country.
4. Our state is made up of smaller areas.
5. You can tell others where you live by naming things nearby.
6. Directions can help you find the place you live.
7. A grid can help you find places.

CHAPTER

1

LOCATING SOUTH CAROLINA

We all live on **Earth. Earth** is shaped like a giant ball. A **globe** is a model of Earth. It helps us see what Earth is like. A **map** is flat. It is a drawing. It shows places on the earth. You can use globes and maps to find your home state. That is what this chapter is all about.

Finding Our Continent

Look at the picture of the globe. Look at the globe in your classroom. A globe shows us where places on Earth are **located.**

We can find South Carolina on a globe. Study the globe. How does it show what parts of the earth are water? How does it show land?

Find the big areas of land on the globe. These land areas are called **continents.** You have to turn the globe to see all of them.

Name the continents you see on the globe.

You can see all of the continents at one time if you look at a map of the earth. A map of the

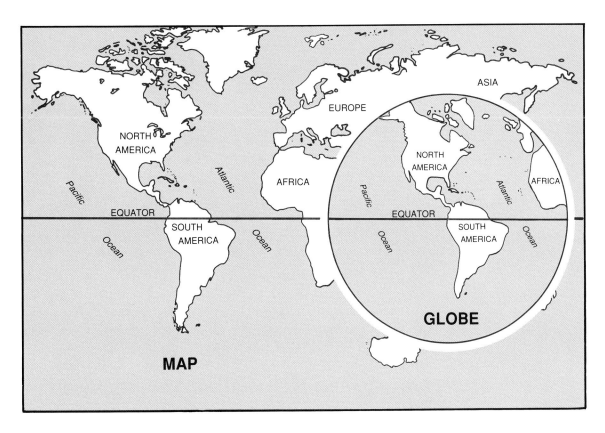

MAP

GLOBE

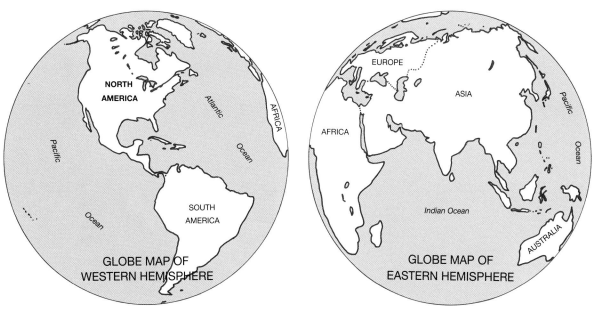

GLOBE MAP OF
WESTERN HEMISPHERE

GLOBE MAP OF
EASTERN HEMISPHERE

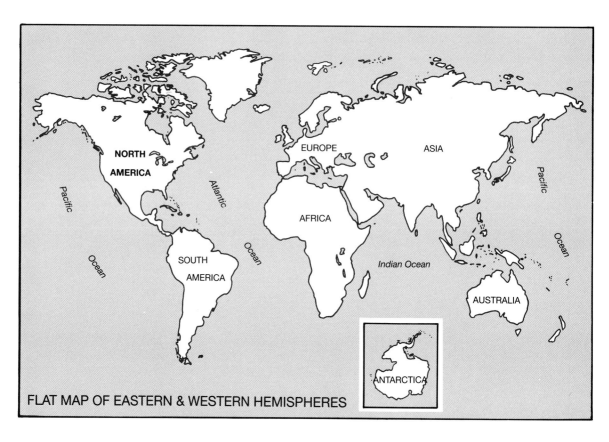

FLAT MAP OF EASTERN & WESTERN HEMISPHERES

4   At Home in South Carolina

earth shows the same area that is on the globe. Name the continents you see on the world map.

We live on the continent called **North America.** Point to it. Trace the edges of it with your finger. What does its shape look like to you? Can you find North America on any globe or world map? Use its shape to help you.

Finding Our Country

North America is a big area of land. It is divided into smaller areas. Each cf these is called a **country.** Our country is called **The United States of America.**

Find the United States on the map of North America. Trace its shape. What other countries are next to our country? What large bodies of water touch it? How would you tell a friend where the United States is?

Finding Our State

Our country is like a giant puzzle. It is made up of 50 pieces called **states.** Each state is an area of land where people live. South Carolina is one of the 50 states of the United States.

Look at the map of the United States. One state is a different color from the others. That is South Carolina.

Many maps do not show South Carolina in a special color. How could you find our state on those maps? Here are three ways to try.

Using Shape

Look at the shape of South Carolina on the next page. Trace it with your finger. South Carolina looks like a rough triangle. (Some say it looks like a piece of pie.) The three sides of the triangle are not straight. They are curvy and uneven. South Carolina has an unusual shape. The shape can help us find it.

Can you draw the shape of South Carolina without looking at a map? Try it. Is your drawing the same shape as South Carolina? Check the map to be sure.

Look at the drawing of South Carolina. Then look at the drawings of the other states.

Which are large? Which are small?

Look at a map of the United States. Which states are large? Which are small?

To find South Carolina, look for a small state shaped like a triangle.

Using Directions

Directions can also help us find South Carolina. On the globe and on the map there are four main directions. They are **north, south, east,** and **west.**

Most maps have direction finders. Some look like this:

Point to each letter. Tell what direction each stands for.

Suppose we drew a big direction finder on our map of the United States. Look at the line that

goes east and west. Put your finger on it. On which side of the line is South Carolina? Good. South Carolina is in the south.

Now look at the line that goes north and south. Put your finger on it. On which side of that line is South Carolina? Good. South Carolina is in the east.

We can put the directions together. The new direction is **southeast.** South Carolina is in the **southeastern** part of the United States.

Using Things Nearby

You can also find South Carolina by its neighbors. South Carolina has two states as neighbors. Look at the map. What state is our neighbor to the north? What state is our neighbor to the south and west, or southwest?

Our state's third neighbor is the Atlantic Ocean. The **ocean** is a huge body of salt water. It is to the east of South Carolina.

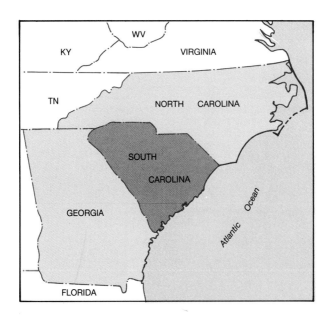

Now you know the name of our continent. You know the name of our country. You also know where South Carolina is. You know some ways to locate our state. On how many different maps can you find South Carolina?

DO YOU KNOW?

Only four of the fifty states have exactly two states as next-door neighbors. South Carolina is one of these four states. Can you find the other three on a map of the United States?

You can learn a lot from place names. Think about the name of our country—the United States of America. The last part tells you where our country is located. How does it do that?

The first part tells you what our country is like. Our country is made up of states which chose to unite, or act together.

Think about the name of our state, South Carolina. It tells you there is more than one state named "Carolina." It says our state is south of the other Carolina.

Can you find other states whose names tell where they are located?

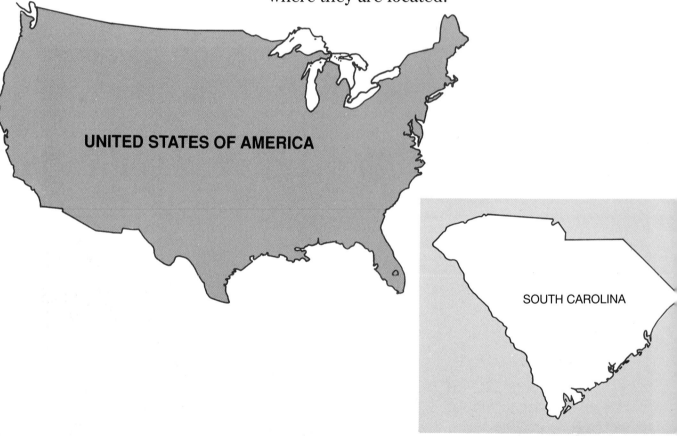

UNITED STATES OF AMERICA

SOUTH CAROLINA

CHAPTER
2
LOCATING
YOUR HOME

You know what South Carolina is. You also know where it is. But do you know where your home is in our state?

South Carolina is made up of many communities. Some are towns. Some are cities. In which kind of community do you live? What is the name of your community?

You can use maps to locate your community in our state. You can use maps to find your street in your community. In this chapter you will learn how to do both these things.

Locating Your County

Suppose you had to explain where you live to someone who lives elsewhere. How could you do it?

One way is to name the part of the state you live in. South Carolina is a puzzle like the United States. But its pieces are not called states. They are called **counties.** A county is an area of land inside a state. South Carolina has 46 counties. Find your county on the map. Trace its shape.

Using Directions

You can use directions to find your home. Look at the South Carolina map with the direction finder. Think about how you used a direction finder in Chapter 1. Use this one the same way.

What two directions tell where your county is? Put the two directions together.

Now you can tell someone where you live.

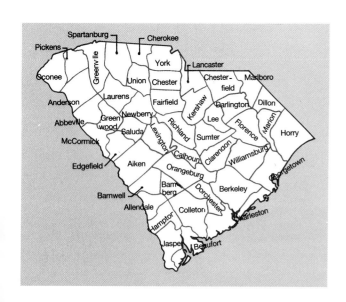

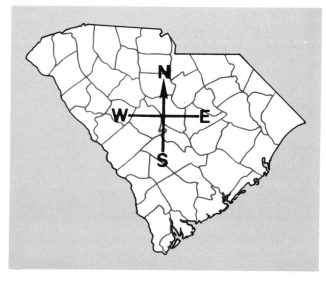

Say, "I live in _____ County in the _____ part of South Carolina."

Using Things Nearby

Another way to explain where you live is to name important or well-known things nearby. Many people know where our largest cities are located. Look at the map. Do you live in or near one of those cities? If so, you can say, "I live (in/near) _____."

Many people know where the main **rivers** are located in South Carolina. Rivers are long streams of flowing water. They flow across the state, heading to the ocean. Some of the rivers join to form **river systems.**

Look at the map. It shows our main river systems. Name them. What rivers are a part of each system?

What river is nearest to your home? Find it on the map. Trace it with your finger. Is it part of a main river system? Which one?

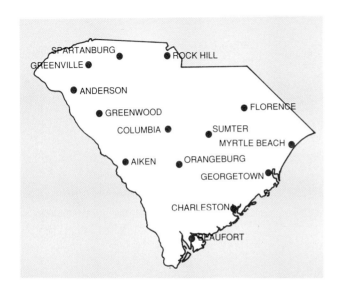

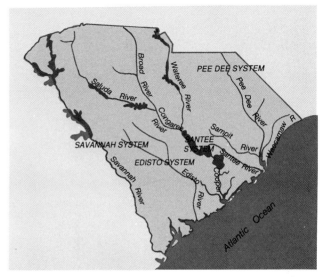

DO YOU KNOW

All rivers flow downhill. That means they all run from high land to low land. Where do you think you will find the highest land in South Carolina? The lowest? How do the rivers tell you?

You can explain where you live by naming this river and its river system. You can say, "I live near the _____ River. It is part of the _____ System."

Locating Your Address

So far you have seen maps of the earth. You have seen maps of the United States and South Carolina. You have used these maps to locate your country, your state, and your community.

Look at this map. What does it show?

How is this map different from the others?

A community map shows streets. You can use a community map to find the street where you live.

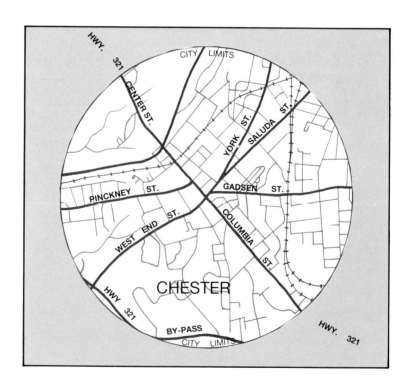

Using a Grid

Look at the map of Moncks Corner. The squares on the map are called a **grid.** Each grid square has a number and a letter.

Find square 3-B. What streets are located there? Suppose you want to find Tram Street. Look in square 4-E.

You can use the grid to find places on this kind of map. Can you find your home on a map of your town or city?

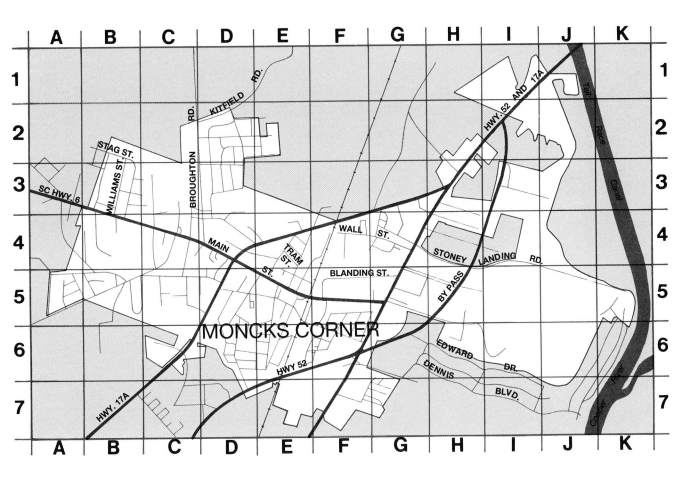

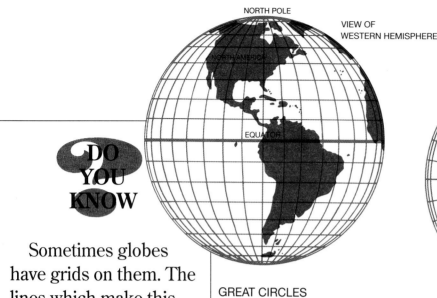

NORTH POLE

VIEW OF
WESTERN HEMISPHERE

NORTH AMERICA

EQUATOR

GREAT CIRCLES
AROUND THE GLOBE

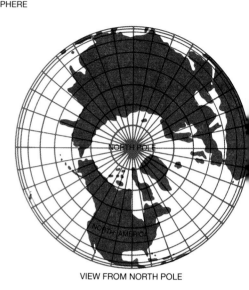

NORTH POLE

NORTH AMERICA

VIEW FROM NORTH POLE

DO YOU KNOW

Sometimes globes have grids on them. The lines which make this grid are called **great circles**. Why do they have this name? Trace one with your finger to see.

How can the globe's grid help us?

Now you know that South Carolina is an area of land on Earth. You can find it on a map. Your home is a place. You can find it on a map, too.

But South Carolina and your home are more than places on a map. You will find out more about them in Unit II.

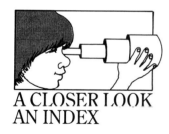

A CLOSER LOOK
AN INDEX

This unit has been about finding places. Sometimes finding a place is easy. Sometimes it is hard.

People use tools to make hard things easier. Many maps have a tool people can use. It is an **index.** It makes finding places easier.

A map index lists the places on the map. It names the grid square where each place is located. It tells you where to look on the map.

An index is an important tool for locating places.

Reviewing Main Ideas

1. Where is South Carolina?
2. What is the shape of South Carolina?
3. How can directions (N, S, E, W) help you find places?
4. Why is it helpful to know places near your home?
5. How can a grid help you find places?

Using New Vocabulary

Think about the new words you have learned. Some words name things made by nature. Some name things made by people. Draw two circles on your paper. Name one circle **Made by Nature.** Name the other **Made by People.** Write each term below in the circle in which it fits best. Be ready to explain your work.

globe	great circle	index
country	river system	map
county	grid	continent
community	state	earth

Can you find another way to group these new words?

Remembering People and Places

Tell why we should remember each of these places:

United States of America   Earth
North America   South Carolina
the southeast   your community

Thinking About South Carolina

1. Put the following words in order by the size of the thing the word names: state, county, country, community, continent. Is your order **always** correct?
2. Make a grid of your classroom that shows where you sit.
3. Which of the following do you think is **most** important in learning about your state: geography, culture, or heritage? Why?
4. Suppose you are moving to Atlanta, Georgia. How could you tell your friends where your new home is located?

Being Creative

Pretend that a pen pal from England has told you that he or she wants to visit you. You think this is a great idea. Write a letter to your pal giving exact directions to your home in South Carolina.

THE LAND

South Carolina is a beautiful state. Its **natural environment,** the land and all the living things on the land, helps make it a good place to live.

Our state has high land and low land. The high land is in an area called the **Up Country.** The low land is in the **Low Country.** In between is an area called the **Midlands.** In this unit you will learn more about the geography of these three areas.

In this unit, you will learn that:

1. The land in South Carolina has been shaped by water, wind, and sun.
2. Our land is always changing.
3. The land is different in the Up Country, the Midlands, and the Low Country.
4. The different environments in our state provide homes for many living things.
5. Plants and animals have features and habits which help them live in certain parts of our state.
6. All of the parts of our South Carolina environment depend on each other.

At Home in South Carolina

SOUTH
CAROLINA

LOW COUNTRY

CHAPTER
3
THE LOW COUNTRY

The Low Country is the part of our state which is closest to the ocean. The land is flat and low.

The Low Country is made up of the **coast** and the **coastal plain.** The coast is the land along the ocean. The plain is an area of flat land between the coast and the middle of the state.

This chapter is about the geography of these two parts of the Low Country.

Low Country Climate

Do you live in the Low Country? If so, you know about the weather there. You also know about the **climate.** Climate is the usual type of weather in an area over a long period of time.

Summers in the Low Country are usually hot. Winters are cool.

Look at the map. What are the usual winter temperatures? What are the usual summer temperatures?

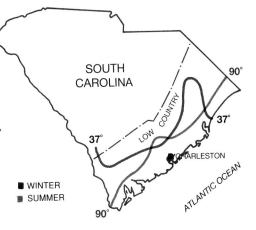

About 48 to 50 inches of rain fall on the Low Country each year. That is enough to help plants grow well. The warm, moist climate is an important part of the environment.

The Coast

The coast is one of the most beautiful parts of South Carolina. Much of it is sandy, white **beach.** Our longest beach is the Grand Strand. It goes from Little River to Georgetown—almost 55 miles. It is one of the longest unbroken beaches in the world.

Have you ever taken a walk on the beach? You are going to take one now. Look at the pictures while you listen.

Pretend you are standing on one of our beaches. You can see the ocean pounding the sand with white-capped waves called **surf.** You can hear the sound of the surf as it meets the shore. The surf is caused by the wind blowing over the top of the ocean. When the wind is calm, the waves are low. When the wind is blowing strong and fast, the waves are higher and rougher.

As you stand on the beach, you see the water coming up higher and higher. In a few hours, more and more of the sand is under water. When this happens, we say the **tide** is coming in. At high tide the ocean covers the greatest part of the beach. After high tide, the tide begins to go out, or **ebb.** Bit by bit more of the beach is out of the water. At low tide the greatest part of the beach is out of the ocean. The tide rises and ebbs two times a day. Which do you think people like better—high tide or low tide?

When the tide comes in, it brings with it seaweed, shells, and small animals. As the tide ebbs, you see that some shells and animals are left behind. You may want to collect shells as you walk on the beach at ebb tide. You may find a **lettered olive,** our state shell. You may also find sea animals like starfish, sea urchins, or a horseshoe crab. If you are lucky, you may even find a sand dollar!

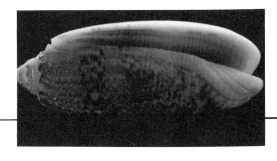

DO YOU KNOW

A sand dollar is not a dollar, a starfish is not a fish, and a horseshoe crab is not a crab. What are they?

Sand Dollar

Starfish

Horseshoe Crab

As you walk on the beach, you see many birds at the edge of the water. Some may be sandpipers. Some may be gulls. They are looking for small shellfish and other animals to eat.

You look out over the water and see some brown pelicans getting their food directly from the ocean. A pelican flies over the water and dives down when it sees a fish. It snatches the fish up in its beak and flies off. The pelican has a pouch in its beak to hold the fish it catches.

As you look over the ocean, you see some large fins in the water behind the white-capped waves. You have spotted a school of bottle-nosed dolphins, or por- poises, mammals that live and feed in the ocean. They must come to the surface now and again to breathe. You can see them when they come near the surface for air and when they play near the shore.

The ocean feeds more than shore birds and sea animals. It also feeds animals that live on the beach. Some of these animals leave their homes in the sand to get food when the tide is in. Then when the tide ebbs, they burrow back into the wet sand and wait for the tide to rise again. The ocean provides food for people, too.

South Carolinians get shrimp, oysters, clams, blue crabs, and fish from the ocean.

As you look away from the ocean at the other side of the beach, you see high piles of sand called **dunes.** The dunes have grasses called sea oats growing on them. The sea oats and other plants help hold the sand. They help keep the wind from blowing the dunes away and the water from washing them away into the ocean.

In August and September big storms called **hurricanes** sometimes hit the coast with heavy rain and high winds. The dunes help protect our coast during the hurricanes. They help keep the rough surf away from the area behind the beach where people live. You can learn a lot from a walk on the beach, can't you?

The Islands

Many **islands** lie along our coast. An island is a small piece of land with water on all sides.

The coastal islands are very important to

South Carolina. Some of our best beaches are on islands.

Some of our islands have stayed wild. These serve as a **refuge** for many birds and other animals. In a refuge the plants and animals are protected from people.

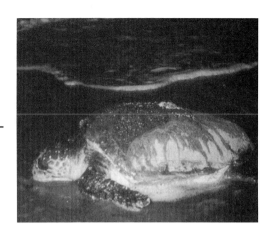

Homes for Animals

Sea islands are important to the loggerhead turtle. Female loggerheads lay their eggs at night in holes they dig in the **dunes.** They cover the holes with sand to hide the eggs.

In two months the eggs hatch. Then the baby turtles make their way across the sand to the ocean.

But few loggerhead eggs become adult turtles. Many are eaten by raccoons. Some may be disturbed by people. That is why a refuge is important for the loggerheads.

Barrier Islands

The sea islands protect our coast from the ocean. The ocean sides of these islands take the pounding of the **surf**. The water between the islands and the coast is calmer and more gentle.

Look at the map of the coast near Beaufort. What islands are located there? What bodies of water lie between the islands and the coast? How will these bodies of water be different from the ocean?

Look at the map of the coast near

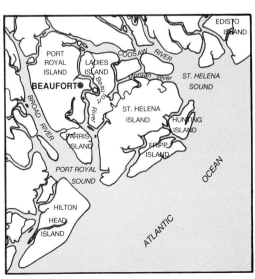

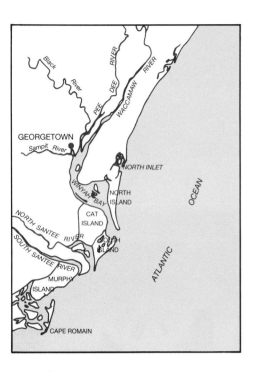

Georgetown. What islands are located there? What protected body of water do you see?

→ Because they protect the coast from the ocean, the islands are called **barrier islands.** South Carolina has more than 150 of them. What do you think would happen if these islands disappeared?

Wetlands

Some areas in the Low Country are called **wetlands.** These low areas are covered by water all or part of the time.

Marshes

Marshes are grasslands which are covered with water. At the coast many are **salt marshes**. They are sometimes called **tidal marshes.** When the ocean is at high **tide,** the salty ocean water floods the marsh. When the tide **ebbs,** ground under the marsh is uncovered.

You are going to take a walk in the salt marsh. Look at the pictures as you listen.

READ TO ME

Pretend you are stepping into a salt marsh at low tide. Your first steps are in thick marsh grass. You bounce gently. The ground feels springy. Water may seep out from under your feet. Roots and other parts of marsh plants make the ground feel like a sponge. You walk toward the muddy area of the marsh. Here there are fewer plants. The mud is very wet and soft. It oozes around your feet. You see small shellfish in the mud. Crabs scurry away from you. Would you like to live in the marsh if you were a crab?

Many animals live and feed in our salt marshes. About two-thirds of our saltwater fish and shellfish spend all or part of their lives in a tidal marsh. Can you name some of them? Many larger animals come to the marsh to find food. Ibis, blue herons, egrets, marsh hens, and other birds feed there. So do animals like raccoons. The salt marsh is the nursery and feeding ground for many ocean and coastal animals.

When the tide ebbs out of the marsh, it takes rotted bits of dead marsh grass out to sea with it. Many of the ocean animals depend on this dead marsh grass for food. You can see why the salt marsh is important in the life of the ocean.

The Low Country also has **freshwater marshes.** These are large, grassy areas, too. But the water in them is fresh. Where do you think the fresh water may come from?

Swamps

Some of the wetlands are **swamps.** A swamp is like a marsh, but it has trees in it. Some people call it a flooded forest.

Our Low Country rivers are known for their cypress swamps. There tall cypress trees stand in black water. You can often tell a cypress tree by the "knees" which stick up from the water around it.

Our freshwater wetlands provide a **habitat,** or home, for wildlife. Here many animals can find the food, water, and shelter they need to live.

DO YOU KNOW

The bodies of waterbirds are made especially for their watery life. What special body part helps the pelican? The heron? What other animals live around water? How do their bodies help them?

Forests and Grasslands

Swamps and marshes are the forests and grasslands of the wetlands. The dry parts of our coastal plain have forests and grasslands, too.

Trees and Other Plants

Many kinds of trees grow in Low Country forests. Close to the coast you find tall **palmetto** trees. They like the warm Low Country climate. They are among the few trees that can live in the salty air near the ocean.

The palmetto is South Carolina's state tree.

Look at the picture. How is the palmetto different from other trees you know?

Another tree that likes the Low Country is the live oak. Live oaks are huge trees with thick trunks and big branches. They are called live oaks because they can live for hundreds of years.

Some live oaks have a gray plant growing in their branches. This plant is called Spanish moss. It makes its food from the air instead of the soil. Spanish moss likes to live in cypress trees, too.

The coastal plain has large areas of pine forest. People have planted many of the pine trees that grow here. Pine trees are **evergreens.** They are green all year long. Most Low Country forests are evergreen.

Many interesting plants live in Low Country forests and grasslands. Two unusual ones are

the Venus' flytrap and the pitcher plant. Both of them eat insects. Did you know a plant could do that?

Animals

Low Country forests and grasslands also provide habitats for many animals. How many of these animals do you know?

Suppose you were one of these animals. Would you like our forests and grasslands? How would you feel if our Low Country forests were cut down? How would you feel if people built houses on the grasslands?

There are many different areas in the Low Country. There are barrier islands, beaches, wetlands, forests, and grasslands. Low Country waters provide habitats for fish and shellfish. Forests and grasslands provide habitats for plants and wildlife.

The Low Country is an important part of South Carolina. Which part of it do you think you like best? Why?

On our coastal plain are large, oval areas called Carolina bays. They look as if a giant fist had slammed into the earth. Some Carolina bays are dry. Others are wet and swampy.

A CLOSER LOOK
CAROLINA BAYS

You can visit a Carolina bay at Woods Bay State Park. It is located where Florence, Sumter, and Clarendon counties join. You can walk on a boardwalk over black swamp waters. You can see alligators, blue herons, and many other animals.

Our Carolina bays are special. You can find them in only three places in the world—South Carolina, North Carolina, and Georgia.

CHAPTER
4
THE UP COUNTRY

The Up Country is the part of our state which is farthest from the ocean. It is called the Up Country because the land is high.

Two areas make up the Up Country. The mountains are in the northwest corner of South Carolina. The rest of the Up Country is called the **Piedmont.** That means the land "at the foot of the mountain." This chapter is about the geography of the mountains and the Piedmont.

Up Country Climate

Do you live in the Up Country? If so, you know about the climate there. The Up Country shows the difference in seasons more than any other part of our state.

In summer Up Country trees are leafy and green. The temperature is hot in the Piedmont, but cooler in the mountains.

In autumn it gets cooler all over the Up Country. The leaves on many of the trees turn bright yellow, orange, and red.

By winter the leaves have fallen off the trees. Temperatures can be quite cold. Sometimes there are ice and snow storms. Usually they do not last long.

In spring new green leaves appear on the trees. The temperatures get warmer and flowers begin to bloom.

Sometimes strong storms called **tornadoes** hit the Piedmont area. A tornado lasts only a short time. But it can do a lot of damage.

Each season in the Up Country is different. Which is your favorite? Why?

The Mountains

Our South Carolina mountains lie in parts of Oconee, Pickens, and Greenville counties. They are part of the Blue Ridge Mountains. When you look at them from a distance, they look smoky blue at the top.

The Blue Ridge are old, old mountains. You can tell they are old because they have rounded tops. When mountains are young, they have sharp, pointy tops. As they grow older, the tops are worn away by rain, ice, sun, and wind. This wearing away is called **erosion.**

After hundreds and hundreds of years, the sharp mountains become rounded like the Blue Ridge. Did you know that mountains grow older just like you?

Water, ice, sun, and wind are still **eroding** our mountains.

DO YOU KNOW

Sassafras Mountain is the highest point in South Carolina. Can you find it on a South Carolina Map? What other mountains in our state are almost as high?

Mountain Forests

Most of our mountains are covered with forests. The mountain forests are different from Low Country forests.

Most of the trees are **deciduous.** Deciduous trees have leaves which turn color in the fall and then drop off.

The main deciduous trees in our mountain forests are oaks. How do these look different from the live oaks of the Low Country?

Many other deciduous trees live in the mountain forests, too.

Have you ever walked through a mountain forest? Let's take a walk now. Follow the pictures as you listen.

Pretend you are walking through one of our mountain forests. It is spring. As you look overhead, you see that the branches of the tallest trees make a kind of ceiling above you. The branches are covered with new green leaves.

At some places the branches fit together tightly. Little sun gets down into the forest. At other places the branches have spaces between them. Here the sun comes through to light the forest. Where there is little sunlight, few smaller trees and plants grow under the tallest trees. Where there is more light, more plants can grow.

As you look around you, you see smaller trees and bushes. You see flowering dogwood trees, a red-leafed red maple, sassafras, some wild blueberry bushes, and many ferns. It is very quiet, but you hear the sound of running water. A mountain stream is nearby. You walk toward it. Near the stream you see bright flowers of mountain laurel and rhododendron which grow near the banks.

At the stream you see the water rushing swiftly over and around rocks. The water moves quickly as it runs down the slope of the mountain. It looks white as it splashes over the rocks. Few plants can grow right next to a stream that moves as quickly as this one. Only plants which attach themselves to the rocks can live here without being swept downstream.

Although our swift mountain streams are hard places for plants to live, they are fine habitats for rainbow and speckled trout. These fish need the cool mountain temperatures. They also need lots of oxygen to breathe. Mountain streams pick up oxygen when the water splashes up over the rocks.

Now you turn and go back through the woods the way you came. You hear the crack of a dried twig as you step. You can feel the sponginess of rotten leaves under your feet. The rotting leaves are turning into a rich, dark soil. You look around you at the plants growing close to the forest floor. You see some bluets growing near the stream. Farther along you find a jack-in-the-pulpit and some pretty violets. Isn't the mountain forest beautiful in the spring?

How will it look in the fall? How will it look in the winter?

Mountain Animals

You have not seen any forest animals on your walk. But many live in our mountain forests.

Birds feed on insects they find in the forest. They are part of the forest **food chain** of eat and be eaten.

Many mammals live in the mountain forest, too. The forest provides the food, water, and shelter these animals need to live.

DO YOU KNOW

Groundhogs, or woodchucks, live only in the mountainous western part of our state. Why do you suppose they like to live there?

Do you remember the story about how the groundhog is supposed to help predict the weather? Do you think the story is true?

The Piedmont

Southeast of the mountains lie the rolling hills and **valleys** of the Piedmont. The valleys are large, low areas. They have been cut out by rivers and streams. The valleys once were shaped like V's. Now they are shaped like U's. What do you think has changed the shape of the valleys?

The soil in the Piedmont is not sandy like Low Country soil. Instead, it is a red clay. Once the clay soil was covered by a layer of rich, dark soil. The dark soil was worn away by erosion.

Streams

Many streams and rivers run through the Piedmont. Where the land slopes steeply, the streams move fast. Where the land is flatter, the streams move more slowly.

If you look at a Piedmont stream, you may see water running swiftly over large rocks. Some of the rocks look greenish. If you touch them, they feel slippery and slimy. They are covered with **algae.** Algae are tiny plants. They are able to hang onto the rocks.

On slower streams you may see some floating plants. On the edges of these streams you may see some rooted plants.

At one time large areas around Piedmont streams were covered with tall cane. These areas are called **canebrakes.** A few large canebrakes can still be found. Some people like to use cane poles for fishing.

Piedmont Habitats

The Piedmont has many kinds of land. There are fields and forests. There are also some swamps and marshes, grasslands and bushy areas.

Here and there are large pieces of bare rock. Sometimes a small mountain rises higher than the rest of the hills.

Many interesting animals live in the Piedmont. Look at the pictures as you hear about some of them.

Some Piedmont animals prefer to live near marshes, swamps, and streams. You may see their tracks in the damp earth. The muskrat, mink, and river otter make their homes in the area. So does the beaver. Beavers cut down small willow and birch trees near a stream. They use the wood and mud to build a dam on the stream. The water in the stream backs up to form a pond. What parts of the beaver's body do you think help make it a good builder and a good swimmer?

Other animals prefer grassy fields and the bushy areas around the fields. Bobwhite quail, for example, like to make their nests on the ground. First, they find a spot under a fence or bush. Then they make a hollow for their nest and line it with dead grass.

Tall grasses, briers, and other field plants provide food and shelter for many small mammals, too. Jumping mice, meadow voles, striped skunks, and cottontail rabbits are just a few of the animals you can find there.

When there are also trees at the edge

of the field, you may find opossums. These unusual mammals have special tails which allow them to hang upside down from tree branches. Female opossums have pouches in which they carry their babies.

Many interesting animals live here, don't they?

Forests

The Piedmont has fields and wetlands. It also has several kinds of forests. Some are

evergreen. These are made up mostly of pine trees.

Other forests are deciduous. The main trees are oak and hickory. Flowering trees grow there, too. So do sweetgum trees.

Sweetgum trees make a gummy, golden sap which some people like to chew. In the fall the tree forms prickly balls containing seeds. These drop off onto the ground.

Just like the mountain forests, our Piedmont forests are important. They provide a habitat for wildlife. They make rich soil. And they help hold the soil so that it is not so easily eroded.

DO YOU KNOW

Over half of South Carolina is covered with forest. Some of our forests are protected by the government. Is there a state or national forest near your home? Why do you think we protect our forests?

The Up Country is an interesting part of our state. It changes with each season of the year. Some of the land is mountainous. Some is hilly. And some is lower down in valleys.

Some areas are rocky. Some areas are covered with fields and forests. Other areas are covered with swamps and marshes. The different kinds of land make habitats for many kinds of plants and animals.

How is the Up Country different from the Low Country? In what ways are these two parts of our state alike?

Raven Cliff Falls

Have you ever seen a waterfall? A waterfall is made when part of a stream cuts way down into rock. The water from the upper part of the stream then has to "fall" down to the lower part of the stream.

A famous South Carolina waterfall is named Issaqueena Falls. A legend says the falls

A CLOSER LOOK
WATERFALLS

got their name from an Indian girl named Issaqueena. She fell in love with an Englishman. The Indians threatened him and Issaqueena ran to warn him. She fell over the falls. Some say she was never seen again. Others say she landed on a ledge behind the falling water. What do you think happened to her?

A CLOSER LOOK
LEGENDS

Legends are stories that have been retold through the years. Many people have retold them. Often people have changed the stories to make them more interesting.

There are many legends about the land in South Carolina. One of them is about Table Rock. People say that a great Indian Chief used the flat rock as a table. And he used the mountains around Table Rock as stools.

Do you think the legend is true?

CHAPTER
5
THE MIDLANDS

A narrow strip of land lies between the Up Country and the Low Country. It is called the Midlands. The Midlands area is in the middle of our state.

The Midlands is a little like the Up Country. It is a little like the Low Country, too. And it is different from both. This chapter is about the geography of this land in the middle.

Land in the Middle

Do you live in the Midlands? If you do, you know that it is an interesting area. It has rolling hills and valleys. It also has flat lowlands. It even has a few small mountains. It has red clay soil and loose, sandy soil. It has wetlands (marshes and swamps) and open fields. Which of these things are like the Up Country? Which are like the Low Country?

The climate of the Midlands is in the middle, too. The Midlands can be hot in summer. But it

does not get as hot as the coast. The Midlands can be cold in winter. Sometimes there may be ice or snow. But it is not as cold as in the Up Country. You could say the Midlands has an in-between climate.

Both deciduous and evergreen trees grow in the Midlands. You can find both Up Country plants and Low Country plants growing there.

Yellow jessamine, our state flower, grows in the Midlands and in all parts of the state.

Many Up Country and Low Country animals can live in the Midlands, too. The **Carolina wren,** our state bird, lives here as well as in other parts of our state.

Carolina wrens can live at the edges of fields, in swamps, and in bushy areas. You probably hear them more often than you see them. Their song sounds like "tea-kettle, tea-kettle."

The Midlands is a little like other parts of South Carolina. But it is also different. Only the Midlands has the fall line and the Sand Hills. These make the Midlands special.

The Fall Line

Running through the Midlands is the **fall line.** At the fall line the high land of the Piedmont drops down to the low land of the coastal plain. North and west of the fall line, the land is hard and rocky. The soil is red clay. South and east, the land is soft. The soil is loose and sandy.

Rivers flow swiftly over the fall line. At some places they have formed waterfalls. These falls give the fall line its name.

At other places the water flows rapidly over rocky streambeds. The water splashes and swirls as it hits the rocks. We call these places **rapids.**

Some places the water is very shallow. It flows around and over bars of sand which the river or stream has built up over the years. The sandbars were formed by the bits of soil which the water carried from higher land. These shallow areas are called **shoals.**

Our South Carolina rivers change when they cross the fall line. Above the line they are swift-flowing and rather narrow. Below the line they flow more slowly. Where the land is very flat, the water may not appear to be moving. But it is. It is being pushed by water coming from the Up Country. In the Low Country the rivers become wider. The water spreads out over the flatter land.

The Old Coast

Long ago the fall line was the coast of our state. Ocean covered the Low Country.

Fossils have shown where the ocean was. Fossils are the remains of plants or animals of long ago. These remains have been saved in layers of rock for thousands of years.

You can find fossils of sea animals south and east of the fall line. Have you ever found one?

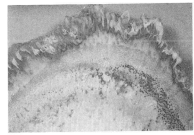

Rivers and ocean shaped the land around the fall line. The rivers brought small bits of soil from the Up Country. They dropped the soil at the old coast. The ocean brought sand. The ocean and the wind built the sand and soil into large dunes. Today we call these dunes the Sand Hills.

The Sand Hills

The Sand Hills are rolling hills of sandy soil. Much of this soil is dry. Water drains out of it

quickly. Only a few kinds of plants can live where there is little water.

Have you ever walked in the Sand Hills? Let's do it now. Look at the pictures as you listen.

READ TO ME

You are standing in a dry area of the Sand Hills. Around you, you see some pine and oak trees. They are growing farther apart here than in the mountains. Between the trees you see areas of sand where few plants grow. These areas of sand and few trees and plants look rather bare. Some people call them **barrens.**

The plants you see around you in the barrens are able to live in drier land. Pine trees can grow here because their roots grow deep and their needles can hold water well. You find another evergreen called rosemary which also grows well here. This is the only place it grows in South Carolina.

On the ground around you, you see many acorns, the seeds of oak trees. When they begin to grow, acorns put out long **taproots.** These thick roots reach deep down into the soil to find water. This is why oaks can grow in the Sand Hills.

All of the small plants you see growing in the sand have special features that let them grow where it is dry. You see thistles all around you. Thistles send their roots deep into the soil. You also see prickly pear cactus growing near you. The prickly pear is a **succulent.** It can store water in its stems and leaves. Did you know that cactus grows in our state?

Plants

Some areas of the Sand Hills are not so dry. There a layer of clay lies under the sand. The clay helps hold water in the soil. In these areas more plants can grow.

One tree you can find there is the persimmon. The persimmon tree produces a fruit which is very sour if it is not ripe. Have you ever eaten a persimmon?

Vines and bushes grow in these wetter areas, too. One is the huckleberry bush. Have you ever picked huckleberries? They look and taste a little like blueberries.

Animals

You may wonder if many animals can live in the Sand Hills. Many do. In fact, the Sand Hills are home for some animals found in few other places in the state.

One of these is the pine barrens tree frog. Another is the red-cockaded woodpecker. These animals need the special Sand Hills habitat.

The red-cockaded woodpecker needs an old pine tree to make its nest hole. It can live only in areas like the Sand Hills where there are old pines.

Both the pine barrens tree frog and the red-cockaded woodpecker are **endangered.** They are becoming rarer. The area where they can live is getting smaller. The Carolina Sand-hills National Wildlife Refuge protects both these animals. You may want to visit the refuge to see many of the Sand Hills animals and plants.

Congaree Swamp National Monument

There is a special place in the Midlands just south of Columbia. It is the Congaree Swamp National Monument. The area is not a true swamp. It is a **floodplain.** A floodplain is a low, flat area beside a river. It is sometimes flooded by river water. The Congaree Swamp is flooded by the Congaree River 8 to 10 times each year. People call it a swamp because that is what it looks like much of the time.

Trees and Animals

The trees in the Congaree Swamp National Monument are very old. Many were already old during George Washington's time.

One pine is 300 years old. (The United States is only about 200!) This old pine is 150 feet tall. It measures almost 16 feet around its trunk.

Many other trees in the Congaree Swamp are the largest of their kind in the United States. Some of the cypress trees even have knees that are over 6 feet high.

The branches of the tall old trees let little sunlight reach the ground. Few new trees can grow in this swamp. They cannot get enough sun.

Some animals live in the Congaree Swamp. But it is especially important as a home for

DO YOU KNOW

At one time buffalo and elk lived in South Carolina. Why do you think they are no longer here?

What other plants and animals are in danger of losing their homes?

birds. Several kinds of birds which are losing their habitats elsewhere have found a good home here.

Like other wetlands, the Congaree Swamp protects other areas from flooding. It takes in the flood waters so they do not need to go elsewhere. The swamp also helps clean the water. Waste and dirt from upstream come into the swamp. The swamp holds the waste and uses it. Cleaner water goes on downstream.

The Congaree Swamp was made a **national monument** by the United States government. A national monument is an area protected and saved for you and your children. Why do you think our country thought the Congaree Swamp was worth saving?

DO YOU KNOW

Only one state in the United States has more of its area covered by wetlands than South Carolina does. Where would you look for it on a United States map? What state do you think it might be?

No neat line divides the Up Country from the Low Country. Instead there is the Midlands. The Midlands is an in-between place. Parts are like the mountains and the Piedmont. Parts are like the coastal plain. But the Midlands is special, too. Only in the Midlands can you find the fall line, the Sand Hills, and some of the oldest trees in the United States.

Some people say the Midlands is a place of changes. Do you agree?

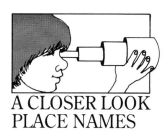

A CLOSER LOOK
PLACE NAMES

Do you go to Silver Bluffs Elementary School in Aiken County? Do you know how your school got its name? It is on a **bluff.** A bluff is a high, steep cliff or river bank. Your school was named for the land.

Many place names come from the land. Kingstree in Williamsburg County was named for a tall pine. Long Cane Creek in the Abbeville area was named for the tall cane there. People said it grew twice as high as a man.

Do you know other places named for the land?

Reviewing Main Ideas

1. How have water, wind, and sun shaped the land in South Carolina?

2. In what ways is our land always changing?

3. Name the three areas of our state. Tell a way each area is different from the other two.

4. How is the Midlands like the other two areas?

5. Why do you find different plants and animals in each part of the state?

Using New Vocabulary

Think about the new words you have learned. Draw two circles. Name one circle **About Animals.** Name the other **About Environment.** Write each term below in the circle where it fits best. Be ready to explain your thinking.

refuge   salt marsh   fall line
beach   hurricane   tornado
endangered   rapids   sand hills
barrier island   habitat   dunes

Can you find another way to group these words?

Remembering People and Places

Tell why we should remember each of these places:

Congaree Swamp   barrier islands
Piedmont   Sassafras Mountain
Carolina bays   old coast

What other places do you think we should remember? Why?

Thinking About South Carolina

1. If you could live in any other area of the state, which one would you choose? Why?
2. What if there were no rivers in South Carolina? How do you think life here would be different?
3. How is the climate different in the three parts of our state? What climate do you like best? Why?
4. Nature has changed our land over the years. What changes do you think will happen in the future?

Being Creative

Pretend that you meet a loggerhead turtle, a beaver, and a red-cockaded woodpecker. They are young and they are lost. Each one asks you where to build a home in South Carolina. Write down what you would tell each of them. Give them all the help you can!

EARLY HISTORY

South Carolina has not always been a state. At first it was just an area of land. It stretched from the ocean to the mountains. At that time it was not called South Carolina.

In this unit you will learn how South Carolina became a state. You will learn about the first people who lived here. And you will learn how people came here from other countries. You will learn how these people made South Carolina a state.

UNIT 3

In this unit, you will learn that:

1. Many groups of people lived here before people came from other countries.
2. White and black settlers came to South Carolina from many parts of the world.
3. The natural environment affected the way people lived.
4. Different groups sometimes had trouble living together on the land.
5. The settlers helped form a new country.

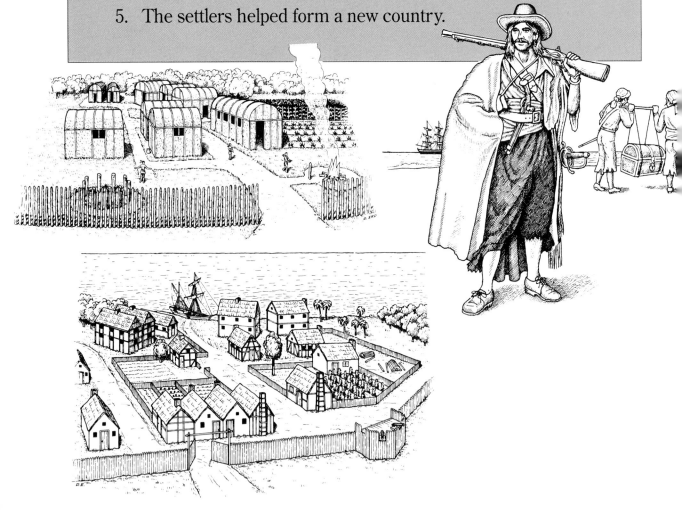

CHAPTER
6

FIRST SOUTH CAROLINIANS

The first people to live in South Carolina were **Native Americans.** They lived here long before people came from other countries. Sometimes they are called **Indians**.

We will call these people the **First South Carolinians.** They were the first to live in our state. This chapter is about these First South Carolinians and how they lived.

Where They Lived

The first South Carolinians belonged to different groups, or **tribes.** Each tribe had its own name.

Each tribe lived in a certain area of South Carolina. The members of the tribe spoke the same language. They had the same **customs,** or ways of doing things. Their language and customs held the tribe together.

The tribes were different from each other. They had different languages and customs.

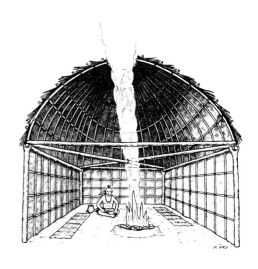

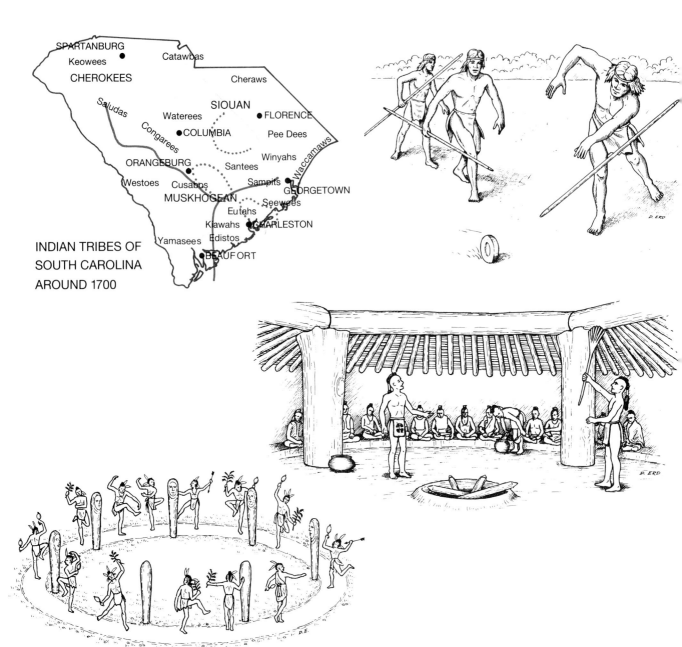

INDIAN TRIBES OF
SOUTH CAROLINA
AROUND 1700

Some tribes were large and had many members. Their tribal lands covered large areas. Most tribes were small and had fewer members. These tribes lived in smaller areas of our state.

Look at the map. It shows where the different tribes lived. Find where you live today. What tribe or tribes lived near you? Can you tell which tribes were largest?

Homes

The First South Carolinians lived in all parts of what is now our state. Usually they lived near a river or the ocean. Why do you think they lived near water?

Some of the tribes lived in the Up Country. Others lived in the Low Country. The homes of Up Country tribes were different from those of the Low Country.

The First South Carolinians built their homes from materials they found around them. They built homes that would be comfortable in the climate of their area.

Low Country Homes

The coastal tribes built their homes of bark. They warmed long poles in a fire so they would bend. Then they put the poles in the ground in a circle.

They bent the tops together and tied them with bark or moss. The poles made the frame of the house.

When the frame was built, the Indians covered it with bark. The bark made the house waterproof. The homes had to be strong to keep standing in strong winds and rainy weather.

Up Country Homes

The mountain tribes had to build warmer homes. Usually they built their homes in a rectangle shape. They used logs or branches for the walls. Then they covered the walls with clay. Why do you think they needed to use the clay?

The Up Country forests had the trees the mountain tribes needed for their homes. The Up Country soil had the clay. Sometimes the Indians used a weak paint on the red clay. They made it from white clay or oyster shells.

Villages

All South Carolina tribes built towns or **villages.** These were groups of homes and buildings the tribe used for meetings and **ceremonies.** (A ceremony is a kind of special event. A wedding is a ceremony. Can you think of others?)

In some villages the buildings were laid out along streets. Some towns had walls of logs around them. We call this kind of wall a **palisade.** The palisade helped protect the village and the tribe members.

The First South Carolinians were loyal to their tribes. The tribe was important in their lives. Each tribe had a **council.** The council was a group that helped make decisions for the tribe.

Every tribal village sent a person to **represent** or stand for them in this council. The council was led by a **chief.** But all the **representatives** in the council voted on things that affected them.

In each tribe there were smaller groups called **clans.** The clans were large families. They often had animal names. A child belonged to the clan of the mother, not the father. The mother's brothers helped raise the child. The father belonged to a different clan. He helped raise his sister's children.

D. ERD

DO YOU KNOW

A child of the First South Carolinians had the family or clan name of the mother. Are our naming customs the same as those of the First South Carolinians?

What They Looked Like

Have you been wondering what the First South Carolinians looked like? The first white settlers described the Indians they saw. The First South Carolinians looked tall and healthy. Their skin was reddish brown. They had long, black hair.

The members of many tribes had flattened heads. They thought the flattened head looked nice. They also thought it made them better hunters.

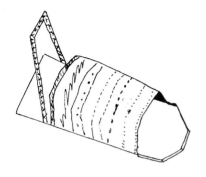

To give their children flattened heads, they tied each baby to a **cradle board.** The babies were on cradle boards for about a year.

The First South Carolinians made clothing from animal hides and skins. What kinds of animals do you think they used? Sometimes the coastal tribes wove Spanish moss into something that looked like a grass skirt. Later, after the white settlers came, the Indians traded for cloth which they used for clothing.

Food

The First South Carolinians were hunters and farmers. They either hunted for or grew all their food.

Maize, or Indian corn, was the main **crop** they grew for food. They ate it at most meals. They used maize to make bread. First they put the corn **kernels** in a hollowed log. Then they used a heavy stick to pound the kernels into corn meal. It took almost half a day to grind the corn to make enough bread for one day.

The Indians also made **hominy** from maize.

They took the skin or hull off the kernels. Then they dried the kernels. When they were ready to eat the hominy, they boiled the dried kernels in water.

Sometimes the Indians ground the hominy into a white meal called **grits.** How do you think they fixed grits?

Besides maize the Indians grew beans, peas, squash, and other garden vegetables. They gathered fresh nuts and fruits which they found around them.

The Indians got meat by hunting and fishing on their tribal lands. They had no way to store food. So they had to hunt and fish in the winter when crops could not grow. What kinds of meat do you think they ate? Which tribes do you think may have eaten more fish and shellfish?

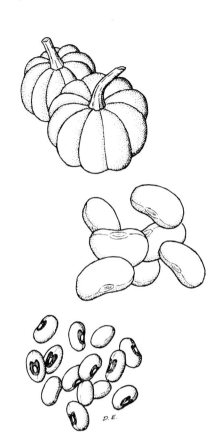

Fun

Do you like to play and have fun? Do you like music and games? Most people do. The First South Carolinians did.

Their favorite games were contests. They liked to win. Often they bet on who would win the contest.

Music was important then, too. The First South Carolinians had their favorite music. But their instruments were different from ours.

They made rattles by filling turtle shells and gourds with stones. They made drums by covering hollow logs with animal skins.

Going Back In Time

Historians, people who study the past, can learn a lot from looking at one person's life. Often they study a person by looking at pictures. Sometimes they read things the person has written.

We do not have writing done by the First South Carolinians. But we do have drawings which show how they lived. We know what settlers said about them. We can imagine how one of the First South Carolinians must have lived.

In your mind, go back to the time before black and white settlers came. Imagine you are listening to an Indian boy named Little Fox tell about his life.

I'm Little Fox and I am a member of the Edisto tribe. We live along the coast.

There are many other tribes besides the Edisto in South Carolina. Most are peaceful, but some are warlike and we have to be careful of them.

My village is on the edge of a great forest. I helped build our home. My father cut the poles from cedar trees. Cedar, like hickory and pine, will get tough when warmed in a fire, yet it will still bend. It also smells good.

We always keep a fire going inside our home. There is a hole in the roof to let the smoke out. We like the fire during the cold weather. During the summer the fire makes the house very hot, but that does not matter. It helps keep the insects away.

Like most other villages, our town is surrounded by a wall. Outside the wall are large fields that are owned by the tribe. Everyone in our village works in these fields. We share the maize that we grow there. My family also has a small garden, but Father does not help there as he does in the large fields.

Our only tools are ones that we make. I help tie stones to sticks to make tools to break up the hard ground. Shells and animal bones tied to sticks also make good tools. Getting a field ready to plant is hard work, and it takes a long time.

I would rather hunt than work in the fields, so I am glad when winter comes. My uncle is the best hunter, and he's teaching me. I can't always kill an animal with one arrow as he does, but I will be able to do that one day. I am good with a blowgun and can almost always kill small animals with it.

I like to hunt for deer and bear. Mother is always glad when we kill these, because their skins can be used for clothing and their meat is good to eat. Bear oil helps keep the bugs off, so I rub it all over me. Mother puts it on my baby sister's skin to toughen it. Father uses bear oil as a decoration whenever there is a special ceremony.

My grandfather taught me how to fish. He sometimes uses a net, but he prefers to fish with a hook tied to a pole with a string. I like to shoot the fish with an arrow. That way I feel like I am hunting. But I don't catch as many fish that way.

My family's home is near the center of the town. The council house is nearby. That is convenient for my father who is a member of the tribal council. Our council house is the largest in any Edisto town and it seats over one hundred people. When the council meets, the town is full of visitors, and we have games and contests for days.

The men's favorite game is called "chunky." Someone rolls a large stone, and all the men throw their spears at the point where they think the stone will stop rolling. My father can usually put his spear at the exact spot where the stone stops. He is always the winner. I'm going to watch him so I'll be able to do the same thing one day. I'm already one of the best stickball players among the children.

Mother has just made a new moss skirt to wear to the Fox clan's ceremonial dance. She is a member of the Fox clan, so my sister and I are also. That is how I got my name. At the dance, mother and other women will wear turtle rattles strapped around their legs. My grandfather will beat the drum. All the dancers will circle around, the men on the outside and the women on the inside. The children usually dance in another circle nearby.

Yesterday a large ship stopped off shore. Some men led by a Captain Sandford came to our town. They were from England and one of them, a Dr. Henry Woodward, wanted to stay with us. Why are these men coming to our land? We have heard stories about other ships. None of the people from the other ships have stayed long, but what if they did? What if they wanted to build a town here on our lands? What would happen to me and my tribe? The Edistos have always lived here. We do not want our way of life to change. I hope they do not come back.

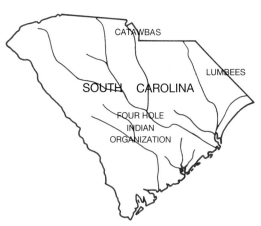

South Carolina Indians Today

Over twenty different tribes once lived in South Carolina. Today members of only three Indian groups live here.

Most of the tribes left the state long, long ago. Some of them fought with other tribes. When they lost, they had to move. Many tribes left when the new settlers came. Some of the tribes disappeared altogether.

There are three major groups of Indians left in South Carolina today. What groups are shown on the map?

The Four Hole Indian Organization is not a tribe. But its members have Indian **ancestors.** Earlier members of their families were Indians.

Do you know a member of one of these Indian groups? Do you have Indian ancestors?

Gilbert Blue is the chief of the Catawba tribe living in South Carolina. His grandfather and his uncle were chiefs before him. Today Chief Blue is helping the Catawbas keep their customs. He tells others about the life and history of his tribe.

**People
Places
Things**

Cherokee Friendship Dance

Chief Gilbert Blue

The First South Carolinians were people like us. They built homes and towns here. They used what they found and grew on the land for food, clothing and tools. How else were they like us?

The First South Carolinians were also different from us. They spoke different languages. They had different customs.

Suppose you had been one of the First South Carolinians. What would you have liked best about life back then?

People search for pottery left by the First South Carolinians.

The Catawba were great artists. They made beautiful pottery. Some Catawbas still make pottery the old way.

The Catawba use clay from river banks. They roll the clay into snake-like coils. Then they build their pottery with the coils. They smooth the pottery with a shell.

They cover the pottery with wood chips. Then they bake it in an open fire. The chips give the pottery color.

When the pottery is baked, they polish it with a smooth stone. Making this pottery takes time. Would you like to make pottery like the Catawba?

A CLOSER LOOK
CATAWBA
POTTERY

D. ERD

CHAPTER
7
NEW SETTLERS

The Indians lived alone in South Carolina for hundreds of years. Life changed when explorers and settlers came from Europe.

An explorer is a person who travels to an unknown area to see what is there. **Explorers** from Spain, France, and England visited South Carolina. Many tried to start **settlements,** or new towns. This chapter is about the explorers and settlers who came to South Carolina.

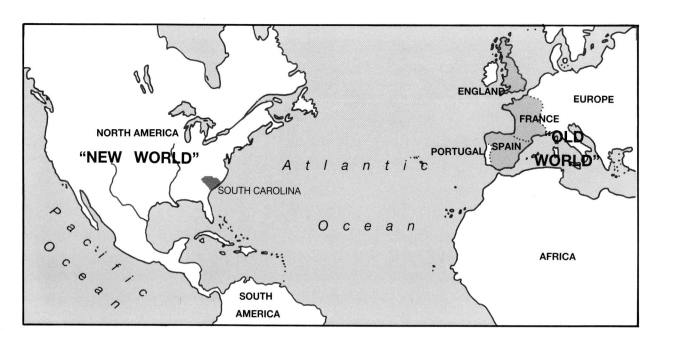

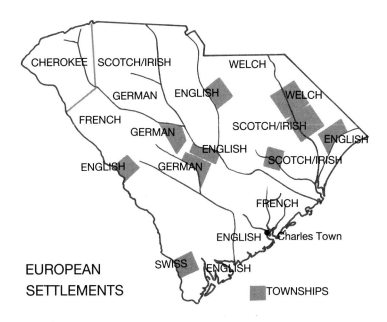

CHEROKEE · SCOTCH/IRISH · WELCH · GERMAN · ENGLISH · WELCH · FRENCH · SCOTCH/IRISH · GERMAN · ENGLISH · ENGLISH · ENGLISH · GERMAN · SCOTCH/IRISH · FRENCH · ENGLISH · Charles Town · SWISS · ENGLISH

EUROPEAN
SETTLEMENTS

TOWNSHIPS

European Explorers

The Indians were the first South Carolinians. All of the people who came to our state after them came from other countries.

When the explorers came, they **claimed** all the land they saw. They said the land belonged to their country. Some of the early explorers built forts and tried to start towns. Why do you think they did that?

Spanish explorers were first to come to South Carolina. Over 350 years ago the Spanish started a settlement near Georgetown. It did not last long. The settlers returned home. Other Spanish settlements on Parris Island near Beaufort also failed.

Later the French started a settlement near Beaufort at Port Royal. This settlement failed, too. The settlers returned home.

Monument to Charlesfort on Parris Island

There are many reasons why these settlements did not last. The settlers were not used to living here. They did not know how to live on the land. Some caught diseases and died. Some fought among themselves. Some fought with the Indians. The settlers who stayed alive were ready to go back home. And they did.

Very little is left to tell us about these early settlements. Even their names are gone. Later settlers renamed the areas when they came and stayed. All we have to remember these early visitors are monuments that have been built where the settlements were.

DO YOU KNOW

A stone called the Pardo Stone is in the Spartanburg Regional Museum. It has the date 1567 and other carvings on it. These may have been made by early explorers.

Suppose the explorers did carve the stone. Why might they have done it?

A Permanent Settlement

The first to start a settlement which lasted, or was **permanent,** were the English. Charles II was the King of England. English explorers claimed land in the New World in his name. King Charles said the land was his. He could do whatever he wanted to do with it.

He owed money to eight of his noblemen. Instead of paying them money, he gave them land in America. They became known as the **Lords Proprietors.**

The Lords Proprietors named their land Carolina. They wanted to honor King Charles whose Latin name was Carolus. The land included what we now know as North and South Carolina and Georgia.

Left: George Monck, Duke of Albemarle
Right: William, Earl of Craven

Sir George Carteret   Sir William Berkeley   Lord John Berkeley

DO YOU KNOW?

Some places in South Carolina are named for the Lords Proprietors. How many can you find on a South Carolina map?

Top: Edward Hyde, Earl of Clarendon
Bottom: Anthony Ashley Cooper, Earl of Shaftesbury

An English Colony

The Lords Proprietors sent a group of settlers to Carolina. These people were to start a **colony.** A colony is a settlement far away from the home country.

The settlers were supposed to build their new settlement at Port Royal. When their ship landed, an Indian chief told them of another spot to build their town. They looked at both locations. Then they chose the one the chief had told them about. Find it on the map.

Choosing the location for the settlement was just the beginning. The settlers had to clear the land, build homes, and find food.

These first settlers built homes like those of the coastal Indians. They used sticks, bark, and mud. They also built a palisade around the new settlement.

It takes a long time to clear fields and grow crops. But finding food was a problem the

Albemarle Point, 1670

settlers had to solve quickly. Do you remember Dr. Henry Woodward? He helped the settlers find food.

Dr. Woodward had stayed in Carolina. He had lived with and learned from the Indians. He taught the new settlers how to live in Carolina. Dr. Woodward traded with the Indians to get food for the settlers.

Some say he brought rice seed to South Carolina. Later rice became the colony's first main crop. Without the help of Henry Woodward, this settlement might have failed like the others.

As others came to the colony, the settlers needed a better location for the main settlement. They found a better place down river. The old location became known as Old Town. The new location was named Charles Town. Now known as Charleston, it grew to be an important colonial town.

At the location of Old Town there is now a state park called Charles Towne Landing. If you visit there, you can learn about early years in South Carolina.

A Growing Colony

More and more settlers came to South Carolina. Charles Town was the only town. But people began to build homes outside the town walls.

At first, growing food and building homes kept the settlers busy. Later they started growing rice and **indigo,** a plant that makes a blue dye.

These became **money crops.** These were crops the settlers could sell back in England.

Trade

The settlers earned money in other ways, too. They sold **lumber** which they got from the forests.

Some traded with the Indians for skins and furs. Selling the skins and furs in England made many **colonists** rich.

Trading with the Indians helped the colony. But it also caused problems. The Indians got guns for their furs. More and more settlers came and took land from the Indians. The Indians fought back. Many people were killed. Before long, most of the Indian tribes left the area. They went where there were no settlers.

New People, New Towns

More and more people came to Carolina. The land around Charles Town became crowded. Some of the settlers moved away from the coast. They moved towards the Midlands and the Up Country. There they built new towns.

Look at the map. It shows the first nine towns built away from the Charles Town area. Do you live near one of these towns? Are the towns still there? Do they have the same names today?

Some of these first nine towns were settled by people from places other than England. Settlers came from Germany, France, Scotland, Ireland, and Switzerland, too. Many of them wanted **religious freedom,** the right to worship as they pleased.

The French Huguenots were people who wanted religious freedom. Some came to

Carolina and settled near Charles Town. These settlers and others helped the colony grow.

Carolina grew to be a large colony. Then it split into two parts—North Carolina and South Carolina. South Carolina grew fast. It became an important colony.

A Diary

Historians want to know how people felt about living in the colonies. They want to know what it was like to see the colony grow and change. Some of the colonists kept **diaries.** In their diaries they wrote about things that happened to them. We know a lot about early South Carolina from diaries and other records.

Suppose there was once a boy named John Williamson. Suppose he was one of the first to come here from England. Suppose he kept a diary. What do you think he might have written? Listen to what he might have said.

READ TO ME

August 10, 1669

I'm on my way to Carolina. We are starting what Father thinks will be a great adventure. Mother is not sure. She knows what life is like in England, but she is afraid of what our lives will be like in the New World. Our family will get 450 acres of land: 150 acres for Father and 100 acres each for Mother, my sister, Elizabeth, and me. That is more land than we would ever be able to have in England.

Mother was frightened when she first saw the ship. Father is a sailor himself, so he was not surprised. He was happy when we were assigned to the Carolina. He says that he likes the looks of this ship better than the other two. Elizabeth and I do not care what the ship looks like. We are excited.

It was a little sad to see our homeland get smaller as the ship sailed away from the harbor. Mother was crying and so were some of the other women. Father tried to comfort her. He knows the trip will be hard on her and on us, but he decided the chance for a new life in a new land was worth all the dangers. At times Mother said she and Elizabeth should stay in England. She said they could join us after Father and I had built us a home. Father said that it would be too dangerous for them to travel alone, so we are all going to Carolina together. Father and I are looking forward to the new adventure. I can hardly wait to get there.

We will not be the first Europeans to live in Carolina. Explorers from England, as well as some from France and Spain, have been there before. Some of them even tried to start towns, but their towns did not last. Our town will last. We are going to Carolina, and we are going to stay.

February 1, 1670

The trip is much harder than we thought it would be. Mother is convinced that we should have stayed in

England, and I think Father really agrees with her. He never says that he wishes we had not come, but many others aboard the ship do. We have had many storms and the ship is so small. There seem to be people everywhere. It took us forty days to reach Barbados. The food we brought with us almost ran out before we got there. The first part of our trip was bad, but the worst part came after we left Barbados.

We left England with three ships, the *Carolina*, the *Albemarle*, and the *Port Royal*. When we stopped in Ireland to pick up more people, no one joined us and some of our people even left. In Barbados the *Albemarle* wrecked in another storm. That storm was so bad that I thought our ship would be lost also. Fortunately, it stayed together. The *Port Royal* wrecked in another storm when we stopped in the Bahamas. A new ship called the *Three Brothers* joined us there. Now the *Three Brothers* has disappeared. These storms have been terrible. They have already cost us three ships and several lives. The *Carolina* is now sailing alone.

An interesting thing happened when we stopped at another island called Nevis. A man named Henry Woodward joined our party. I like to listen to him talk about his life. He first went to the New World with Captain Robert Sandford. When an Indian chief suggested that his nephew go back with the explorers, Dr. Woodward stayed with the Indians. He says that he learned much from them and enjoyed living in the area where we are going. His stories about the land are wonderful. I am getting excited about our trip again. I had almost lost hope during all of those storms. Things are looking better now. Dr. Woodward says we should be in Carolina soon. Everyone is anxious to get there. I think everyone, including me, wants to be off this ship for good.

May 21, 1720

It is hard to believe that I have lived in Carolina for fifty years. There was nothing here when we arrived. We had to make everything. Our wool clothes were too hot for summer. Then winter was much colder than we thought it would be. Some of our people died, and some went back home. But we stayed.

It was hard, but we built a good colony. Mother never did like it here. She died not long after we moved from Old Town to Charles Town. When I married,

my wife helped make a home for Father and Elizabeth. Father died during the yellow fever epidemic in 1699 along with my wife and Elizabeth's two children.

We were fortunate that our home survived the great fire. A third of Charles Town did not. Then that terrible hurricane almost wiped out the rest of the town. We again proved how strong our colony was. We rebuilt and continued to grow.

I'm fifty-eight years old now. South Carolina sure has changed. There are other towns along the coast and even some inland. One of my sons is a printer here in Charles Town. He is doing well. My other son has moved to Dorchester. He is so far away that I rarely see him. My grandchildren will probably live even farther inland if the **government** can move the Indians out. When we first came, the Indians were friendly. These days the colony is having much trouble with them. Since we both want the same land, I guess we always will have trouble getting along.

There is much talk about ending the Lords Proprietors' rule over the colonies. Many people want the King to take over and make South Carolina a **royal colony.** The Lords Proprietors promised each of the original settlers land in the colony. My family was to receive 450 acres. We never got that much, so I feel no loyalty to them at all. I hope the King will take more control over South Carolina. I wonder what the next fifty or hundred years have in store. My grandchildren will be the ones to see that. I have surely seen my share of changes.

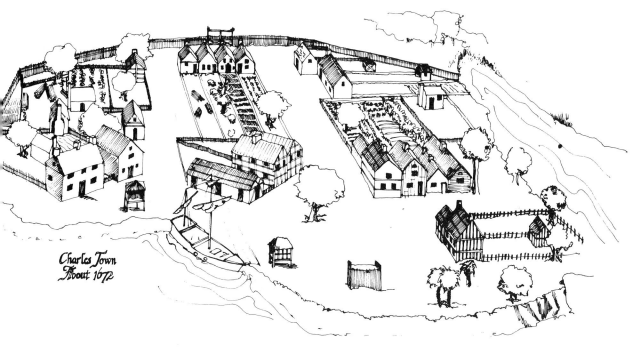

Charles Town
About 1672

New settlers from Europe brought many changes to South Carolina. They cut down forests. They built new towns and farms. They forced most of the Native Americans to leave the area.

Settling the New World was hard. The trip across the Atlantic was dangerous. Living here took hard work. Many died from diseases and in fights with Indians. Why do you suppose people wanted to come here anyway? Would you have wanted to come with the early settlers?

Often we think of explorers as people who lived long ago. But there are explorers today. Some are **astronauts.** They are explorers of space.

A CLOSER LOOK
EXPLORERS TODAY

One South Carolina astronaut was Charles Duke from Lancaster. He walked on the moon.

Ronald McNair from Lake City was the second black person to go into space. He was killed when his spaceship exploded.

Exploring the unknown is exciting. But it has risks and dangers, too. Can you find the names of other astronauts from South Carolina? Would you like to be one?

CHAPTER

8

MAKING A STATE

At one time our state was a colony of England. It was one of thirteen English colonies. Can you find the names of all thirteen?

The thirteen colonies wanted to become **independent,** or free of English rule. They fought a war to have their own country. This war is called the **American Revolution.**

This chapter tells about the Revolution in South Carolina. It tells how South Carolina became a state.

A Royal Colony

The Lords Proprietors had promised land to the settlers. They gave some land, but not as much as they had promised. The people of Carolina were tired of being ruled by the Lords Proprietors. They wanted the King to rule Carolina.

The Lords Proprietors expected to get rich from their colony. They didn't. In fact, they had to spend more and more money on the colony. They wanted to get rid of Carolina. They sold it back to the King. Carolina became a royal colony.

Low Country Plantations

Under the King's rule, South Carolina grew quickly. People built fine homes in Charles Town. They started large farms, called **plantations.** There they raised money crops. Many people became wealthy.

Rice was the first money crop in South Carolina. It grew well in the swampy, hot Low Country. It grew in flooded fields. The fields had to be flooded and drained as the rice grew. This made growing rice hard work. Many of the **planters** used **slaves** to grow the rice.

Indigo

Eliza Lucas helped make indigo an important crop. Her father put her in charge of two plantations. (She was only 16 years old!) She planted some indigo seeds he sent her. She used the leaves from the plant to make the dye. She sold the dye to cloth-makers in England. This made indigo a money crop.

Like rice, indigo was hard to grow. The dye was hard to make. Planters used slaves to work in the indigo fields and make the dye.

Because Low Country planters made money on their crops, they were able to build fine homes. Some of the Low Country plantation houses are still standing.

The Up Country

Traders traveled from the Low Country into the Midlands and the Up Country. They followed Indian paths or trails. They traded goods with the Indians.

Settlers followed the traders to the Midlands. They started towns. Some settlers moved farther away from these towns into the Up Country.

Settlers from other colonies came to the Up Country, too. Some came from Virginia. Others came from Pennsylvania.

DO YOU KNOW

Some Low Country people thought indigo would keep away an evil spirit called the "plat-eye." They put indigo dye around the doors and windows of their homes.

How do people today try to keep away bad luck? How do they try to get good luck?

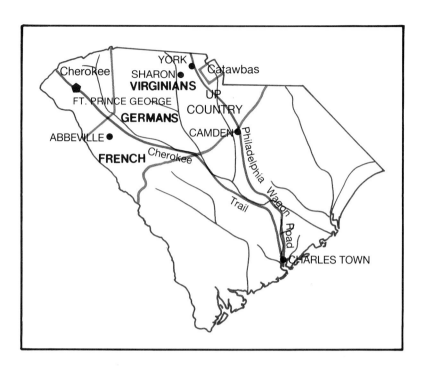

The Up Country settlers cleared land for farms. These Up Country plantations looked different from those in the Low Country. The planters here raised corn, sweet potatoes, beans, and peas. Some raised wheat and barley. Many raised pigs, or hogs. Up Country farmers had no big money crops.

Letters

Historians learn a lot about life in the past by reading letters. We have many letters written by people who lived in South Carolina long ago. Suppose you had a pen pal who lived in the royal colony of South Carolina? What do you think your friend would say?

Pretend you have two pen pals. One is Sarah Thompson from Charles Town. The other is David Campbell from Lancaster. Listen to letters these two might have written to you.

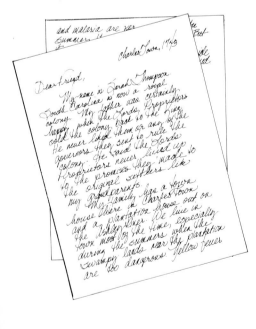

88   At Home in South Carolina

Charles Town, 1743

Dear Friend,

My name is Sarah Thompson. South Carolina is now a royal colony. My father was certainly happy when the Lords Proprietors sold the colony back to the King. He never liked them or any of the **governors** they sent to rule the colony. He said the Lords Proprietors never lived up to the promises they made to the original settlers like my grandparents.

My family has a town house here in Charles Town and a plantation house out on the Ashley River. We live in town most of the time, especially during the summers when the swampy lands near the plantation are too dangerous. Yellow fever and malaria are very bad in the summer. It is hot in town, but it is safer here.

Charles Town is a pretty town. There are nice wide streets made of **cobblestones.** Cobblestones are large rocks used as weights for empty ships. When a ship is empty, it floats too high in the water, and rocks must be used to weigh it down. When the ships return to England, they are carrying rice, furs, and lumber. These provide enough weight, so the cobblestones can be left here. Someone decided that the stones would make a good covering for the streets, and they certainly do. Now when it rains the streets are not muddy.

Our new house is only one room wide. It is turned with the side to the street. Father doesn't have to pay as much in **taxes** as he would if the house faced the street. The long porches on the side of the house catch the breezes and keep the house cooler.

Out on the plantation, Father has been growing rice. He has many slaves to do the work. He says he is going to try planting indigo. He thinks he will make more money, even though he will have to buy more slaves. It will be interesting to see how Miss Lucas's indigo grows on our land. I am looking forward to going back out to the plantation.

Your Friend, Sarah

Lancaster, 1757

Dear Friend,

I'm David Campbell. My family has just arrived here from the colony of Pennsylvania. My parents came from Scotland. They had to leave their homeland in order to worship as they pleased. First they went to Ireland, then they came to America. I was born in Pennsylvania, but my parents felt we would be safer in Carolina, away from the terrible Indian wars.

We are Scots-Irish. A large group of us came here together. We named our settlement Lancaster after the area we came from in Pennsylvania. Our minister says that, as soon as we can, we will build a church and school here.

We chose our farmland carefully. Father wanted land on a hillside near a creek. Flooding is not as bad near a creek as it is around a river. The soil is very rich, and we found a spring on the hillside. Now we do not have to dig a well. We have a lot of land to clear this winter so we can be ready to plant in the spring.

Mother is not happy about the house we put together. Soon we will build a log house like we had in Pennsylvania. Right now an open cabin with three sides and a roof is the best we can do.

I wish we could clear the fields of all the tree stumps. Plowing would be so much easier if the stumps were gone. One of our friends was fortunate to find some fields that had been cleared and used by the Indians. We are going to plant food crops and corn. Father has already planted the apple and peach trees so we will be able to make cider and brandy.

Charles Town is a long way from here. The **royal governor** wants us to obey his laws and even travel all the way to Charles Town for courts and business affairs. That is too far away. And what difference does it make anyway? The people in Charles Town do not care about us out here. Most of them are rich and live in comfortable houses. How could they possibly understand life here in the Up Country?

Your Friend, David

The American Revolution

South Carolina was ruled by England for many years. England made the colonists pay special **taxes.** The tax money went to the English **government.** The colonists had no say about this.

The English King sent **governors** to rule the colonies. These governors were not always good men.

In South Carolina many people were tired of English rule. They wanted to have a say in their own government. They wanted the colonies to become a free and independent country. These people called themselves **Patriots.**

Other people were still loyal to England. They wanted South Carolina to stay a royal colony. These people were called **Tories** by the Patriots.

Signing the Declaration of Independence

The Tories called themselves Loyalists. That is because they were loyal to England. The Tories called the Patriots "Rebels." Do people still call each other names? Why?

The people of South Carolina were divided. When the war started, the Patriots fought the English, or British. They also fought their fellow South Carolinians.

Pretend you have two pen pals from that time. Listen to what they might write about the war.

READ TO ME

Charles Town, 1776

Dear Friend,

People in my family are Patriots. We want South Carolina and the other colonies to be free from England. My father is an **officer** with Colonel Moultrie. Moultrie's men are defending Charles Town. They are afraid the **British** will try to capture the town and regain control of South Carolina. They can't let that happen.

My Uncle Andrew lives in the Up Country. Some of his neighbors still support the King. They burned down his house at night because Uncle Andrew is a Patriot. All of his family could have been killed, but the Tories did not care. How can anyone still support the King after all the things he has done to us? I do not understand why all the people in South Carolina are not working to become free from England.

Your Friend, John Huger

Lancaster, 1776

Dear Friend,

People in my family are Loyalists. We are not going to war against England. The planters in the Low Country may be having problems with the King, but the King has never done anything to hurt us.

If we joined this fight, we might lose our land grants. The King could get angry and cause the Indians to go to war against us. This is not our fight. Why would anyone want to be free from England? We owe the King and England our loyalty.

My father is the leader of a group of Loyalists who are helping keep South Carolina a part of England. I know they have burned some of our neighbors' homes. They had to do that. I'm sorry we have to fight each other in South Carolina, but that is the way it will have to be. We must stay loyal to the King. I do not understand why anyone in South Carolina would want to be free from England.

Your Friend, Thomas Campbell

The War in South Carolina

Many **battles** of the Revolution were fought in our state. One of the earliest was fought in Charles Town.

Colonel William Moultrie led South Carolina's

soldiers. He built a fort on Sullivan's Island. It was made of palmetto logs.

The British fired **cannons** at Fort Moultrie. The cannon balls stuck in the soft palmetto logs. They did not explode or hurt the fort.

Colonel Moultrie and his men held off the British. Charles Town was safe for a while.

The flag Colonel Moultrie's men used was the same color as their uniforms. In one corner was the crescent moon from their hats.

During the battle, the flag fell. Sergeant William Jasper jumped over the wall and picked up the flag. He placed it back over the fort. Then he gave three cheers and returned to safety.

Today our state flag is like the flag Colonel Moultrie's men used. A palmetto tree has been added in honor of the palmetto fort.

The palmetto fort is gone now. But there is still a Fort Moultrie. This fort was built in later wars. But it is at the same place as the palmetto fort.

DO YOU KNOW

Jasper County was named for Sergeant Jasper. Other places in our state were named for **heroes** of the Revolution. Read about some of those heroes at the end of the chapter. How many places can you find that have their names?

General Daniel Morgan

On July 4, 1776 the **Declaration of Independence** was signed. The colonies said they were free and independent. The words were nice. But fighting continued for six more years before they came true.

Winning the War

The British won many battles. They thought that South Carolina was defeated. They were wrong. The Patriots would not give up.

At King's Mountain, the Americans won an important battle. A large Tory army went to King's Mountain. Mountain men from North Carolina, Tennessee, and Kentucky came to help the Patriots. They were good shots. They would not give up. The Tories **surrendered**. The Americans proved they could win a big battle.

At the Battle of Cowpens the Americans won another big victory. Together General Andrew Pickens and General Daniel Morgan of Virginia defeated a large army.

Pickens used a trick to win. He let only a few men shoot at one time. He told his men to aim at the **officers** first. They did, and many officers were killed. Then the British soldiers ran away.

South Carolina helped win the war by keeping the British busy here. The British could not join the rest of their army fighting George

Washington in Virginia. The divided British army had no chance of winning.

Becoming A State

At last the war ended. The British left. Many Tories left with them. South Carolina was independent of England. It became a state and elected a new governor. The people had a say in their own government.

South Carolinians not only formed a new state. They helped to form a new country. **Representatives** from South Carolina helped plan the government for this new country, the United States.

Andrew Pickens

Winning independence was very important to many South Carolinians. They wanted to rule themselves. Many were willing to fight for that. After fighting hard battles, the Patriots won. South Carolina became a new state in a new country.

What do you think would have been best about living here during the Revolution? What would have been worst?

Andrew Jackson

Andrew Jackson was the eighth President of the United States. He was also the only President born in South Carolina. His family lived near Lancaster.

A CLOSER LOOK
PEOPLE OF THE
REVOLUTION

During the Revolution Andrew and his brother, Robert, were captured by the British. An officer told Andrew to clean his boots. Andrew said no. The officer hit Andrew across the head with his sword. The blow gave Jackson a permanent scar.

The two brothers were sent to a prison near Camden. There they became very ill with smallpox. Their mother came, and the British let her take her sons home. Robert died on the way. Andrew was sick for a long time afterwards.

Francis Marion

Francis Marion was called "the Swamp Fox." He fought in the swamps of the Pee Dee. He fought hard. Then he ran away to get his men together. That way he could return to fight on another day. A British officer once said, "Nobody could find that old fox in these swamps."

Thomas Sumter

Thomas Sumter was called "the Gamecock." He was a fierce fighter, but he was careless.

Once he surprised the British. He captured men and supplies. Then he became careless. He and his men stopped by a creek. He knew the British would be following them. But he felt he had found a good hiding place. He had not. While his men were swimming, the British attacked. They killed or captured most of the

men. Sumter escaped, but he lost his men and supplies.

Kate Moore Barry

Kate Moore Barry of Walnut Grove Plantation was a **scout** for the Patriots. Mrs. Barry often took messages to General Daniel Morgan.

One night she had an important message to deliver. There was no one to watch her children. Using a sheet, she tied one of her children to the bed post to keep him safe while she was gone. Then she delivered the message.

Rebecca Motte

Mrs. Rebecca Motte was forced out of her home by the British. They turned her house into their **headquarters.** General Francis Marion planned to burn the British out of the house. Mrs. Motte gave him some fire arrows to use. She was willing to burn down her home to defeat the British.

Mrs. John Thomas

Mrs. Thomas was visiting two of her sons in a British prison at Ninety-Six. She heard the Tories say they were going to attack Cedar Springs camp while the Americans slept. Two of her sons were in this camp near Spartanburg. Mrs. Thomas rode to warn them. Because of the warning, the attack was not a surprise. The Tories were defeated.

Rebecca Motte

Mary Musgrove

Mary Musgrove turned her home into a hospital after the Battle of Musgrove Mill. There and on the battlefield, she treated both Patriots and Tories.

Others

Many men and women in South Carolina helped in the Revolution. What people of the Revolution are famous in your area?

Reviewing Main Ideas

1. Describe the life of the First South Carolinians.
2. What new settlers came to South Carolina? Why did they come?
3. How did the settlers get along with the First South Carolinians?
4. Was life easy for the settlers? Why or why not?
5. Why did the colonists and the British go to war?
6. How did the Revolution change South Carolina?

Using New Vocabulary

Think about the new words below. Arrange them in three groups so that each word fits in only one group. Name the groups. Be ready to explain your thinking.

tribe	plantation	√Tory
village	√explorer	√colonist
clan	revolution	palisade
√Patriot	√slave	settlement

Can you think of another way to group these words?

Remembering People and Places

Many South Carolinians were important in our history. Remember the people you have studied. Pick one whom you admire most or one who is most like you. Write a paragraph that explains your choice.

Thinking About South Carolina

1. How was the life of a First South Carolinian different from your life?
2. Why did the First South Carolinians and early settlers have trouble living close together? Could they have solved their problems better? How?
3. Why was life on a Low Country plantation different from life in the Up Country?
4. How do you think our life today would be different if there had been no American Revolution?

Being Creative

Think about the time of the Revolution. Suppose you had lived then. What part do you think you might have played in the war? Write a story about your adventures in the American Revolution.

LATER HISTORY

South Carolina continued to grow after the Revolution. Our state and country started new governments. Ways of living changed.

In this unit you will learn how South Carolina grew and changed. You will learn how our people began to rule themselves. You will learn how our state fought in a war against other states. And you will learn how our state has changed since that war. You will meet people who have helped our state grow.

UNIT 4

CHAPTER

9
The Young State

10
Civil War

11
Growth and Change

In this unit you will learn that:

1. South Carolina and the United States set up new governments.
2. A new money crop brought changes to South Carolina.
3. Slavery became an important part of life in South Carolina.
4. Our state went to war to keep its way of life.
5. After the war, ways of life changed.
6. Many South Carolinians have helped our state grow and change.

CHAPTER
9

THE YOUNG STATE

South Carolina became a state. It had its own government. South Carolinians **elected,** or voted for, state leaders. They also elected people to represent them in the new United States government.

South Carolinians now had two governments to make rules for them. Sometimes the two governments disagreed.

This chapter is about the young state of South Carolina. It tells why our state disagreed with the United States.

New Governments

When they were free, the new states did two things. They set up a government for their new country, the United States. And they set up governments for themselves.

Do you know what a government does? It makes rules, or **laws,** for people to follow. And it makes sure people follow or **obey** the laws.

Why do people need laws? Can you think of

some laws you have to obey? What would happen if there were no laws?

The United States Government

After the war, the United States needed a government. Each state sent representatives. The representatives wrote the **Constitution of the United States.**

The Constitution told who would make laws for our country. It told who would carry out the laws. And it told who would decide if people disagreed about the laws.

We still have the Constitution today. The United States government is still set up the same way.

The group of people who make laws is called the **Congress.** States send representatives to Congress. These representatives make the laws.

Each state has two U.S. senators. Each state has a different number of U.S. representatives. Large states have more. Small states have fewer.

DO YOU KNOW

The letters "U.S." make a short name, or abbreviation, for the name of our country. Sometimes we use "U.S." and sometimes we use "U.S.A."

Do we have a short name or abbreviation for South Carolina? What is it?

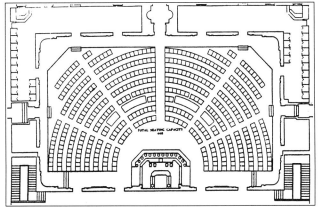

U.S. House of Representatives

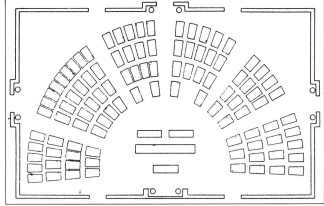

U.S. Senate

George Washington

Woodrow Wilson

Judge Matthew Perry

A person called the **President** carries out the laws. The President is the leader or chief officer of our country.

George Washington became the first President. What President was born in South Carolina? Who is the President now?

The U.S. **Supreme Court** and other courts settle disagreements. **Judges** in the courts decide who is right when people disagree about the law.

Congress, the President, and the Supreme Court are in Washington, D.C. Our country built Washington for the new government. It is the capital city of the United States.

The U.S. government makes laws for our country. The people in all of the states must obey these laws.

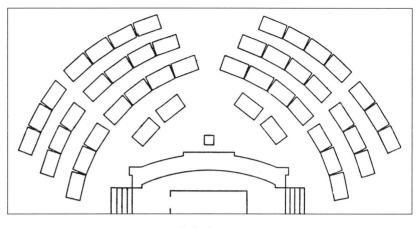

S.C. Senate

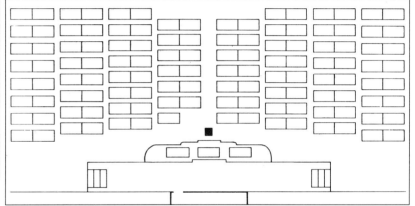

S.C. House of Representatives

South Carolina Government

South Carolina needed a new government, too. Just like the U.S., our state wrote a constitution. The S.C. constitution said laws would be made by the **General Assembly.** The General Assembly was a group of people elected by South Carolinians.

South Carolinians elected the General Assembly. But not all South Carolinians could vote. Only white men who owned land could vote then. Who can vote in our state today?

The General Assembly made laws for our

young state. It also chose a governor, or chief officer, to lead the state. It chose judges for the courts. And it chose our U.S. senators.

Just like the U.S., South Carolina built a new capital city for the new government. It was called Columbia.

The new capital was small at first. It had two main streets, Assembly Street and Senate Street. Why do you think those names were chosen? Other streets were named for heroes of the Revolution. Sumter and Marion were two of them.

The General Assembly needed a place to meet. So South Carolina built a **state house.** It was made of wood. The General Assembly met in this first state house for over 70 years.

DO YOU KNOW

Our first state house looked a little like the White House in Washington. The White House is where our U.S. President lives. The two buildings are alike for a good reason. They were planned by the same man.

Two Ways of Life

Right after the war there were two ways of life in our state. Some South Carolinians had large plantations. The planters raised money crops like rice and indigo. Much of the work was done by slaves. At first most of the plantations were in the Low Country.

Other South Carolinians had small farms. These farmers grew crops for their families to eat. Sometimes they had crops left over to sell. The work on the farms was done by the farmer and his family. At first most of the small farms were in the Up Country.

But soon things began to change. South Carolina planters found a new money crop. This was cotton.

Cotton

The early settlers knew cotton would grow well here. But growing cotton for sale took many workers. Cotton grows in a cluster called a **boll.** In the boll are many small seeds. The seeds must be taken out before the cotton can be sold. It took many slaves to pick the seeds out of the boll. So growing cotton for sale was costly.

Then Eli Whitney invented the **cotton gin.** This machine separated the cotton **fibers** from the seeds. Whitney got the idea for his machine

SHORT FIBER COTTON

from a cat's paw. He saw how the cat's claws could be like a comb. His cotton gin had claws to comb the cotton away from the seeds. The cotton gin made cotton a good money crop.

But there is a big problem with cotton. As it grows, it makes the soil less **fertile.** It wears out the soil. Suppose cotton is planted in the same field year after year. What will happen to the soil?

Keeping the fields fertile was a problem. As the land wore out, planters moved to new land. They started new plantations in the Midlands. And they started plantations in the Up Country.

Soon there were plantations all over the state. All parts of the state had a money crop—cotton. It was called "King Cotton" because it was so important to our state.

As plantations spread, the parts of our state became more alike. The state became united for the first time.

Our state changed in other ways, too. New towns appeared. New roads were built. New schools were started.

Schools

In those days schools were different from schools today. Not everyone went to school.

Often young children were taught at home. The parents might pay a **tutor** to teach them.

There were a few one-room schools. These schools had one teacher. Children of all ages were in the same room. They did not write with pencils as you do. Often they wrote with chalk on a **slate.** They also wrote with pen and ink. They used **quill pens** made from stiff feathers.

People with money often sent their children to an **academy.** This school was like our high school today.

One early academy was in McCormick County. The Willington Academy was for boys only. The schoolhouse was made of logs. It had two rooms. One was for classes. The other was a **chapel** for worship. The boys lived in small huts while they were at the academy.

DO YOU KNOW

The College of Charleston is the oldest **college** in our state. It was started right after the Revolution. A few years later South Carolina College opened. We know it as USC today. What do those letters stand for? Later the Citadel was started in Charleston. It was to train soldiers. What other colleges does our state have today?

College of Charleston

Old USC, South Carolina College

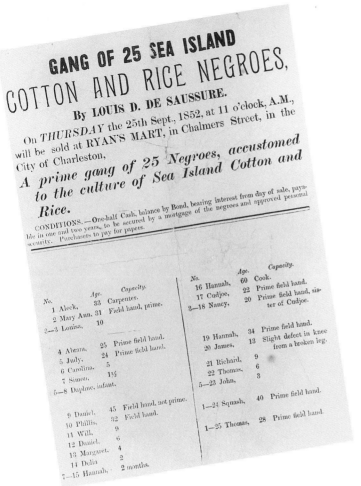

GANG OF 25 SEA ISLAND COTTON AND RICE NEGROES,

By LOUIS D. DE SAUSSURE.

On THURSDAY the 25th Sept., 1852, at 11 o'clock, A.M., will be sold at RYAN'S MART, in Chalmers Street, in the City of Charleston,

A prime gang of 25 Negroes, accustomed to the culture of Sea Island Cotton and Rice.

CONDITIONS.—One-half Cash, balance by Bond, bearing interest from day of sale, payable in one and two years, to be secured by a mortgage of the negroes and approved personal security. Purchasers to pay for papers.

No.	Age.	Capacity.
1 Aleck,	33	Carpenter.
2 Mary Ann,	31	Field hand, prime.
3—3 Louisa,	10	
4 Abram,	25	Prime field hand.
5 Judy,	24	Prime field hand.
6 Carolina,	5	
7 Simon,	1½	
5—8 Daphne, infant.		
9 Daniel,	45	Field hand, not prime.
10 Phillis,	32	Field hand.
11 Will,	9	
12 Daniel,	6	
13 Margaret,	4	
14 Delia	2	
7—15 Hannah,	2 months.	

No.	Age.	Capacity.
16 Hannah,	60	Cook.
17 Cudjoe,	22	Prime field hand.
3—18 Nancy,	20	Prime field hand, sister of Cudjoe.
19 Hannah,	34	Prime field hand.
20 James,	13	Slight defect in knee from a broken leg.
21 Richard,	9	
22 Thomas,	6	
5—23 John,	3	
1—24 Squash,	40	Prime field hand.
1—25 Thomas,	28	Prime field hand.

Slavery

Cotton became more and more important. Planters needed more slaves to grow the cotton. Slavery became very important to plantation life.

Some slave owners took good care of the slaves. But others did not.

Sometimes the owners sold their slaves. Slave families could be separated. Either the parents or the children could be taken away and sold. They might never see each other again. How would you feel if that happened to you?

At Boone Hall Plantation near Charleston you can see a row of slave homes. These nine brick houses were used by the house slaves. Most slaves did not live in houses as nice as those on Boone Hall's Slave Street.

People Places Things

Many people in our country thought slavery was wrong. They wanted to do away with it. They wanted the U.S. government to say no one could have slaves.

Many people in South Carolina wanted to keep slavery. They felt the planters needed slaves. Other southern states agreed. They said each state had a right to do what it wanted.

Not all South Carolinians wanted slavery. The Grimke sisters, Sarah and Angelina, thought it was wrong. The sisters lived in Charleston. They told people slavery was wrong.

Perhaps some people of that time can help you understand the slavery problem. Listen as you hear from two girls. The one is a planter's daughter. The other is a slave. Listen to their feelings about slavery.

Sarah Grimke

Angelina Grimke

Meadowfield
March 1, 1843

My name is Elizabeth Howard. My grandfather moved to Columbia from Charleston. Our home is called Meadowfield. It is one of the largest plantation homes in this part of the state.

We plant acres and acres of cotton. My father says he can sell his cotton for more this year than ever before. He is going to use that money to buy more slaves so he can plant even more cotton next year. The more money he makes, the more I can buy. I like that.

I go to Banhamville Academy in Columbia. It is one of the best schools for girls in the country.

Last week we talked about the Grimke sisters in Charleston. They are saying that slavery is wrong. Not everyone mistreats the slaves. My father treats his slaves well. Slavery isn't wrong.

Charleston
April 25, 1843

My name is Martha. I live in Charleston, but I have just been bought by a planter in Richland County. I'm to be moved to a place called Meadowfield soon, but I don't want to leave my family. Since I was the only one sold, I will be going away all by myself. I will never see my momma and daddy again. Why did Master John want to separate my family? I hope my master will be a kind man.

I hate slavery. Why can't the black people be free like the white people? It would be wonderful to be free. You could go anywhere and do anything you wanted to do.

The new state of South Carolina grew and changed. South Carolinians ran their own government. They also sent representatives to Washington, D.C. Planters found a new money crop. "King Cotton" made slavery more important.

Disagreement over slavery split our country. Most people who wanted slavery lived in the South. Most people who did not want slavery lived in the North. The North and South could not agree.

If you had lived then, what would you have said about slavery?

John C. Calhoun is sometimes called "the greatest South Carolinian." He was born during the Revolution. He went to Willington Academy. Later he became a lawyer.

He was elected to the General Assembly. Then he was elected to Congress. There he became a leader just as he had been in our state.

Later he was Vice-President for seven years. The President at that time was Andrew Jackson.

You can visit Calhoun's home, Fort Hill, in Pickens County. It is in the middle of Clemson University.

A CLOSER LOOK
JOHN C. CALHOUN

CHAPTER

10

CIVIL WAR

The problem of slavery divided our country. Many people in the North wanted to do away with it. The states in the South did not want to change. They did not want the U.S. government to tell them what to do. So the United States went to war.

This war is called the **Civil War.** That is a war in which people in a country fight each other. This chapter tells about South Carolina's part in the Civil War.

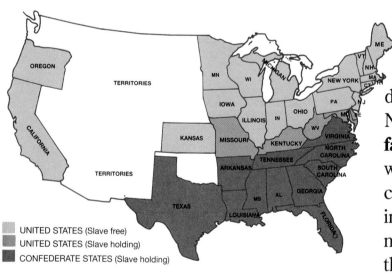

UNITED STATES (Slave free)
UNITED STATES (Slave holding)
CONFEDERATE STATES (Slave holding)

Two Ways of Living

The North and South were different from each other. In the North there were many **factories.** A factory is a building where workers make goods like cloth, shoes, or nails. Machines in the factory help the workers make the goods. Many people in the North made a living from factories. There were farms in the North. But these were small. The small Northern farms did not need slaves.

Many people in the South made a living from farming. Some raised money crops on large plantations. They felt they needed slaves. Other farmers dreamed of having a plantation one day. They felt they would need slaves then.

Some people in the North could not understand slavery. They wanted the U.S. government to say there could no longer be slaves. But the Southern states did not want to be told what to do. The states had a right to decide this for themselves, the South said.

War Comes

Then Abraham Lincoln was elected President. People in the South were afraid he would get rid of slavery. They said the Southern states should leave the United States. They wanted to form a new country.

South Carolina took the lead. Our state **seceded.** That means our state said it was no longer a member of the United States. Other Southern states seceded, too. Together they formed a new country. They called it the **Confederate States of America.**

President Lincoln said no state could secede. He said that once a state was a member of the United States, it was always a member. Lincoln and the U.S. government wanted the Southern

SUNSET VIEW OF FORT SUMTER BEFORE THE BOMBARDMENT.

Jefferson Davis

states to stay in the **Union,** or United States. When the Southern states refused, war broke out.

The very first shots of the Civil War were fired on Fort Sumter in Charleston. Fort Sumter was a U.S. fort. It was on an island off the coast.

Today you can take a boat to Fort Sumter. You can see where the Civil War began.

War in South Carolina

When war broke out, South Carolina was part of the Confederate States. The Confederate President was Jefferson Davis from Mississippi. The leader of the Confederate army was General Robert E. Lee from Virginia.

In the North, Abraham Lincoln was President

Ulysses S. Grant

Robert E. Lee

of the Union. At first several different generals led the Union army. Then General Ulysses S. Grant became the leader.

Most of the early fighting was north of our state. Many South Carolinians fought with General Lee. Many doctors went to be with the army. Our state sent men and supplies to the war. Many started **hospitals** to care for wounded soldiers.

One of South Carolina's most famous generals was Wade Hampton. At first he fought with General Lee. Later he was sent back to South Carolina to help defend the state.

The Blockade

Early in the war the Union set up a **blockade** at Charleston. They sent ships to keep other ships from entering or leaving Charleston.

The blockade kept South Carolina from getting goods people were used to having. Supplies of many things got very low. The people left at home had to save what they had or use other things instead. How would you fix your food if there were no salt? What could you do if you were running out of paper?

South Carolinians did not like the blockade. They used small gunboats to fire on the Union ships. But these did not break the blockade.

DO YOU KNOW?

South Carolina used a **submarine** to fight the blockade. The men in the submarine turned a **crank,** or handle, to make it go. The submarine was very slow. And it could stay underwater only until the air inside was gone.

One man became famous because he got through the blockade. Robert Smalls was a **harbor pilot.** He guided ships in and out of Charleston. He took over a ship called the *Planter.* Then he took the ship through the blockade. By sea he got safely to Port Royal.

Early in the war the Union had captured Port Royal. The Union also took Beaufort and the sea islands in that area. People from the

Robert Smalls

North came to Port Royal and the sea islands. They raised cotton with the help of blacks who lived there. Teachers and **missionaries** also came to help the blacks.

DO YOU KNOW

The Civil War is the first war of which we have **photographs,** or pictures taken with a camera. How can photographs help us understand the Civil War?

The End of the War

Toward the end of the war, the fighting came to South Carolina. General William Sherman led a large army of Union soldiers through the state. General Sherman and his men captured Columbia.

Before Sherman's army left, a fire burned Columbia. Nobody knows for sure who started the fire. Some say Sherman's men burned the city to get even for the war. Others say Wade Hampton's men started it to keep the Union from taking the city. It could have been an accident.

After the fire, only a few buildings were left. People tell many stories about how homes and other buildings were saved.

The old State House was burned. Nothing was left. But a new State House was being built next to the old one. It was supposed to be fireproof. It stood through the fire.

But the new State House had been hit when Sherman's men took Columbia. If you visit the State House, look for the six bronze stars outside. They mark the spots where the State House was hit.

The burning upset many South Carolinians. Some told their feelings in letters and diaries. Listen to two letters that might have been written then.

READ TO ME

Meadowfield
February 17, 1865

Dear Father,

I am writing this letter quickly. Some of General Hampton's men are outside. They have told us that Columbia has fallen to General Sherman's men. We can see fires in the distance.

Mother is frightened about our safety here at Meadowfield since General Hampton's house is nearby. She thinks we should leave, and Hampton's men agree. They said they will try to get this message to you in Virginia. We are leaving Meadowfield and going to Charleston. Mother's old servant, Martha, and her husband, John, are going to go with us. Their son, Joseph, left early in the war.

We all pray you are well and that we will be together soon.

With love,
Your son, Thomas

Virginia
May 6, 1865

Dearest Thomas,

I hope this finds you in Charleston safe and well. I just received your letter of February 17th. We have heard that most of Columbia was burned.

I wish I could come to see about you and your mother. We are still fighting here in Virginia. I don't think this war will ever be over. I am so glad you were not old enough to join the army at age eight, as you thought you were. I have seen many young boys not much older than you die in battle. I hope I'll live to come home, because I fear that the worst has not yet come to South Carolina. If the **Yankees** hated us enough to burn our towns, then what will they do when they win this war? I wish I thought the South could still win, but I don't.

Tell Martha and John that I thank them for staying with us. Take care of your mother. Always remember that I love you both.

Your Loving Father,
Sgt. John Morse

DO YOU KNOW

The North and South had other names for each other during the Civil War. Union soldiers were sometimes called **Yankees.** Confederate soldiers were sometimes called **Rebels.**

The Civil War ended when General Lee surrendered to General Grant in Virginia. Many Confederate soldiers came home to houses that were destroyed. They found fields that had not been tended. Many came home wounded. But some did not come home at all.

After the War

Life changed after the war. People from the North ran the South. Southerners who had fought in the war could not vote. They could not be elected to the government. Many lost their homes and all of their lands.

Times were hard. Blacks and whites had to learn a new way of life. All blacks were now free. The large plantations were gone. There were many small farms, but only a few large ones. People had to find new ways of living.

Suppose you could talk to a South Carolinian about life in our state after the war. What do you think you could learn? Listen to what one South Carolinian might say.

READ TO ME

Meadowfield
June 1, 1872

My name is Thomas Morse. My father returned safely from the war, but many of his friends didn't. My friends, Robert and Andrew, were not as fortunate. Robert's father was killed at Gettysburg and Andrew's father lost a leg at Vicksburg. They both have told me how hard things are for their families.

Times are not easy for us either. Meadowfield was burned after we left for Charleston. When we returned, we moved into one of the slave cabins. So did Martha and John. They stayed with us because they wanted to and because they had nowhere else to go. Their son, Joseph, ran away early in the war. They have heard from him and he is in Boston, Massachusetts. That is a long way from South Carolina.

Early in the war Mother, John, and I had hidden the family silver and jewelry in an old abandoned well back in the woods. Nobody found it, thank God. After the war we had something to sell to pay the taxes on our land. The Yankees who are running the stores in Columbia only gave us a part of what the silver and jewelry were worth. But that was better than nothing.

We saved enough of our land to start

over. Father, John, and I planted the fields. We had to raise enough food for us to eat. Food costs too much to buy, even if you have any money. The fields look good now, but I have never worked so hard in all my life.

We are going to keep our land and start over. When my mother's great-great-great-great-grandfather came to South Carolina aboard the Carolina, there was no house waiting for him. When my father's great-great-great-grandfather came to the Up Country from Pennsylvania, he helped his parents clear the land before they planted their crops. They worked hard, and so can I. Life in South Carolina is going to change, and I am going to change with it.

DO YOU KNOW?

Special grave markers show the graves of men who fought in the Civil War. If you visit an old cemetery, look for a cross with the letters C.S.A. on it. The cross marks the grave of a Confederate soldier.

What do you think C.S.A. stands for?

South Carolina entered the Civil War with high hopes. After four years of war, these hopes were gone. The South was defeated. The state would have to change.

Black South Carolinians had high hopes. The slaves were now free. They could decide to stay in the state or leave. What would you have done? Why?

Many buildings were destroyed when the Union army came through our state. One that was saved was Drayton Hall.

Drayton Hall was built before the Revolution. It is on the Ashley River outside Charleston. During the Civil War Drayton Hall was saved by a disease.

A Confederate officer had moved some slaves into the house. The slaves were ill with smallpox. Many people died from smallpox in those days. That disease made the Union soldiers afraid to go near the house. Drayton Hall was saved.

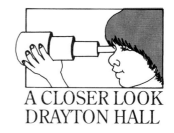

A CLOSER LOOK
DRAYTON HALL

Mary Boykin Chesnut was the daughter of a governor of South Carolina. She was also the wife of a U.S. Senator. Mrs. Chesnut's husband became a Confederate senator after South Carolina seceded.

She and her husband lived on a plantation near Camden. It was called Mulberry. They traveled all over the state. They knew many people.

Mary Chesnut kept a diary. In it she wrote about life in the South. She told about people she knew. Her diary was made into a book. It was called *Diary from Dixie.* Her book helps people understand life in South Carolina before, during, and after the Civil War.

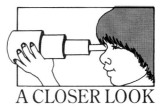

A CLOSER LOOK

CHAPTER
11
GROWTH AND CHANGE

After the Civil War, life in South Carolina had to change. And change it did. Our state today is very different from our state after the war. But the changes did not come easily.

Several big changes stand out. Our ways of earning a living have changed. And the lives of black South Carolinians have changed. The changes have been brought about by many leaders. This chapter is about these big changes in our state.

New Farming

After the Civil War, life changed. The plantations were gone. There were a few large farms in South Carolina. But most of the farms were small. The farmer and his family did most of the work.

Farmers needed many supplies for their farms. They also needed food and clothing for their families. But most farmers had little money. They began to buy on **credit.** They

bought now and agreed to pay later when they had sold their crops. When they could not pay, some lost their land.

Some farmers had land after the Civil War. Others did not. They had to farm someone else's land. They became **sharecroppers.** They had to share their crop with the owner of the land.

Many people left farming. They tried to earn money in other ways. Some went into **business.** Some made a living by selling goods. Others made a living by making goods to sell.

Suppose you could talk to someone who had farmed after the Civil War. Listen to what one of them might have said.

Meadowfield
June 1, 1882

My name is Thomas Morse. Ten years ago today I said I would keep this land. If I had known then what I was going to have to do, I probably would have sold the land and moved to town.

At first we could sell some of the family treasures for food and supplies. But when our treasures were gone, I had no money to buy seed and fertilizer. I had to get these from the store. I agreed to pay the owner after I sold my crops. He charged me twice as much for the supplies I bought on credit as he had for those I bought for cash the year before. I got by until the year my crops were all killed by the drought. No rain for six weeks—my fields were ruined. I had no crops to sell, but I still had to pay the store owner. Fortunately, Mother and Father had enough money to get me through that year.

My wife's brother had a lumber business in the Low Country. He wanted to open a **sawmill** here. He said he would make me a partner if I gave him the land for the mill and my forest lands. I had some land on the Congaree River that was perfect for a factory. The river had enough power to run the sawmill, and my forest lands were close by. We did well in our lumber business.

I am now a businessman rather than a farmer, but my heart will always be in the land.

I have divided my land into smaller farms and have sharecroppers working these farms. I know other land owners who are charging their sharecroppers too much for food and supplies. They are taking too large a share of the crop. I try to be fair to my sharecroppers, because I know how unfair that store owner was to me when I was having troubles. I don't like people who use these hard times and the troubles of others to make themselves rich.

Hard times have to be over soon. Maybe a new day is coming when farmers will be in power once again. I sure hope so.

Help for Farmers

Farmers in South Carolina were very unhappy. They got together. They decided to ask the state government for help.

Benjamin Tillman was a cotton farmer from Edgefield County. He became the leader of the

farmers. He was elected governor of South Carolina. Tillman, "Pitchfork Ben," wanted farmers to have a say in government.

He also wanted to help farmers learn better ways of farming. Tillman started Clemson University as a college for farmers.

"Pitchfork Ben" Tillman (middle), with other farm leaders

Tillman Hall, Clemson University

DO YOU KNOW

Clemson and USC have been playing football against each other for many years. At one time their games were played on a day called "Big Thursday." That day was a state holiday.

Agriculture, or farming, has always been important in South Carolina. Today farmers raise more crops. They use better ways of farming. Some farmers still grow cotton. But there are new money crops.

Textiles

After the Civil War many South Carolinians started new businesses. Some started new businesses to use cotton.

Before the war, planters had sold their cotton to the North or to England. There it was made into **textiles.** Textiles are yarn, thread, cloth, and goods made from cloth.

One South Carolinian had wanted to make textiles here at home. His name was William Gregg. Before the war he built the Graniteville Mill in Aiken County.

Gregg built a town where his workers lived. The town had houses, stores, and churches. Gregg gave the workers a place to work, live, and play. After the war more people built textile **mills.** They also built mill villages for the workers. They had learned a lot from Gregg's ideas.

Many textile villages appeared after the war. The workers' houses were often lined in neat rows near the factory. The Greenwood Mills had the first mill town with brick houses for its workers.

Men, women, and children all worked in the mills. Women were paid less than men. Children were paid the least. They worked 12 hours a day, sometimes for less than 30 cents. They were not allowed to go to school. The work was hard, and the days were long.

DO YOU KNOW

William Gregg was one of the first to worry about children working in mills. He did not allow it. Others later followed his idea. Today we have laws about children working. We have laws that say children must go to school. Is that good or bad? Why?

The mill villages were often away from other towns. So they had things the workers could do for fun. Some of the mill villages had their own teams for baseball and basketball. The teams formed the **Textile League.** They played each other.

There are no mill villages today. Larger towns have grown up around many of them. Today textile workers live like everyone else.

The textile **industry** is still important in South Carolina. But there are many other businesses here, too.

Rights For Blacks

After the Civil War, blacks were given new rights. Black men could vote. They could be in the government. Do you remember Robert Smalls? He became a leader in South Carolina. He became a U.S. Representative from our state. Other blacks also helped in government.

DO YOU KNOW

Claflin University in Orangeburg was started to train black leaders. It was set up by missionaries from the North. Can you name some other colleges that were started for blacks?

But many of the rights did not last. The time after the war left hard feelings between whites and blacks. These feelings lasted a long time. Only in **recent** years have blacks and whites had the same rights in South Carolina.

For many years whites and blacks went to separate schools. They could not go to the same restaurants. They could not go to the same theatres. Black South Carolinians used separate rest rooms. They had to sit at the back of the bus. They were not allowed to vote.

Leaders worked for many years to win rights for blacks. Many groups of blacks and whites tried to work peacefully for the rights of black people.

At last laws were changed. Blacks were allowed to vote. They could be in the government. Blacks and whites began to go to school together. They could go to the same restaurants. They could ride together on buses.

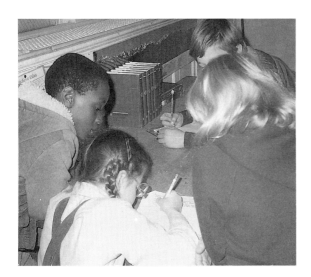

Many South Carolinians did not like these changes. But they happened anyway. They are now a part of our way of life. South Carolina made the changes more peacefully than some other states in the South.

Our state began to have new leaders who were black. Today South Carolina has many black leaders. Who are some where you live?

More South Carolina Leaders

Many South Carolinians have been leaders in our state. Some have also been leaders in our country. Have you wondered about our leaders? Listen to what two of them have done.

READ TO ME

MARY McLEOD BETHUNE
1875-1955

Mary McLeod Bethune grew up in Mayesville. There she worked hard on the farm. By age nine, she was picking 250 pounds of cotton a day. She was eleven before she got her first chance to go to school. Once she started, she never missed a day. She became the best educated person in her community. She helped her friends weigh their cotton and figure how much they owed at the village store.

In those days, poor black children did not usually get much schooling. But Mary was an excellent student. She continued her schooling and grew up to be a famous educator. She first became a teacher in Atlanta. Then in Florida she started a school for black girls. The school became Bethune-Cookman College. Mrs. Bethune was its president.

She became an advisor to presidents when President Franklin Roosevelt asked her to join a committee to help young people. Mrs. Bethune became a friend of Mrs. Roosevelt and visited the White House often.

Mary McLeod Bethune was a leader in black education. She was an advisor to many different presidents.

JAMES F. BYRNES
1879-1972

When James F. Byrnes was young, he was a fine student. But he stopped school at age 14 to earn money to support his mother. He got a job working for some lawyers in Charleston. He learned to take shorthand and record court cases. When he moved to Aiken, he studied to be a lawyer.

With a partner, Byrnes bought a newspaper, but his real love was government. He was elected to Congress. For fourteen years he helped make laws for the United States. When he left Congress, he moved to Spartanburg to practice law. But five years later he went back to Congress as a U.S. Senator. He became one of the most important Senators of his time.

Byrnes was made a judge on the U.S. Supreme Court. That was an important job he could have had for the rest of his life. But President Roosevelt needed him in another job. Then President Truman needed him.

But Jimmy Byrnes' career was not over. When he returned to South Carolina to retire from his years of working for our country, he was elected governor. As governor he served his state well.

DO YOU KNOW

Jimmy Byrnes had to stop school to work after his father died. He did not want other students to have to stop school. He set up **scholarships** that allow many students to stay in school.

How important is school for a leader?

Changes in Government

These leaders of our state grew up after the Civil War. They have seen many changes. And they have helped make some of the changes. Can you name any leaders in South Carolina today?

Our government has changed since the Civil War. We still have the General Assembly to make the laws. We still have a governor to carry out the laws. We still have courts to decide disagreements about the law.

But many more people can vote today. Both blacks and whites can vote. Both men and women can vote. Young people can begin to vote when they are 18 years old.

The General Assembly no longer picks our U.S. Senators. The people elect them. The General Assembly does not pick our governor. The governor is elected by the people.

Maybe you will be a leader in South Carolina. You will know how things have changed in our state. You will find ways to make things even better.

South Carolina has grown and changed since the Civil War. People are finding new ways to make a living. Black and white South Carolinians are learning to work together. Many leaders—black and white, men and women—have helped our state grow. They have helped our country, too.

Our state is always changing. How do you think it will change by the time you are grown up?

After the Civil War a change was made in our S.C. government. A law said the governor had to live in Columbia all year long. But there was no place for the governor and his family to live.

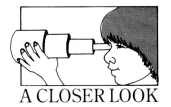

A CLOSER LOOK

There was a house on Arsenal Hill. It had been part of a military academy. The academy had burned with the rest of Columbia. But the house was saved. It became the Governor's Mansion.

There was a vegetable garden with the house in those days. There were also cows, horses, chickens, and a mule for plowing.

Do you know who lives there today?

UNIT 4 REVIEW

Reviewing Main Ideas

1. Why were new governments needed after the Revolution?
2. How was the new South Carolina government like the new United States government?
3. How did cotton and the cotton gin change the way of life in our state?
4. Why did the North and the South go to war?
5. How did life in South Carolina change after the Civil War?

Using New Vocabulary

Think about the new words below. Arrange them in two or three groups so that each word fits in only one group. Name the groups. Be ready to explain your work.

fibers	laws	Rebel
General Assembly	Congress	blockade
Confederate States	boll	state house
Yankee	Union	judge

Can you think of other words that can go in your groups?

Remembering People and Places

Tell why we should remember each of these:

William Gregg   Robert Smalls
Grimke sisters   John C. Calhoun
Fort Sumter   Benjamin Tillman

If you could add one person or place to this list, what would you add? Why?

Thinking About South Carolina

1. How is Columbia different from other cities in South Carolina? Suppose the capital were moved to another city. How do you think Columbia would change?
2. If you could go back to any time since the Revolution, what time would you like to visit? Why?
3. Suppose the South had won the Civil War. How do you think life in our state would be different today?
4. What do you think has been the most important change in our state since the Civil War? Why?

Being Creative

Nobody knows for sure who started the fire that burned Columbia. Pretend you were a detective back then. Write a story about how you solved the mystery of the fire.

UNIT 5

RESOURCES

Have you been wondering why South Carolinians lived the way they did? Have you wondered why some things happened the way they did?

The **resources** in our state help explain this. Resources are things people use to help them make and do other things. Some are **natural resources** like water, land, trees, and minerals. They come from our natural environment. Others are **human resources.** These are people and their ideas, inventions, and work.

In this unit you will learn how South Carolinians have used their resources. You will learn how people invented, made, and used new ways of doing things.

In this unit you will learn that:

1. Our natural and human resources have affected how South Carolinians live.
2. The ways South Carolinians use their resources have changed over the years.
3. Our human resources have influenced how we have used our natural resources.
4. We need to conserve and protect our resources.

CHAPTER
12
WATER RESOURCES

Water is one of our most important **natural resources.** People cannot live without water. People need to drink water each day to stay alive. How many other ways do people use water?

Our state has a good supply of water. South Carolina gets about 95 days of rain each year. The rain fills lakes, rivers, and streams. This chapter tells how South Carolinians have used this water and the waters of the Atlantic Ocean.

Indians Use Water

The First South Carolinians used the water from springs, streams, and rivers. They drank it. They used it to grow and prepare food. And they fished, washed, and swam in it.

Sometimes the tribes used bodies of water as **boundaries.** Rivers and streams became borders between areas used by different tribes. For example, the Broad and Catawba Rivers separated the Cherokee from the Catawba. Look at the map of South Carolina. Do we use bodies of water as boundaries today?

The First South Carolinians also used rivers and streams for transportation. They made canoes, called **dugouts,** from cypress or pine logs. They used fire and shells to dig out the center of a log to make the dugout.

Indians used dugouts to travel. Sometimes they traveled to trade. The dugouts then had to be big enough to carry goods as well as the Indians.

Sometimes the Indians traveled to go to war. Then the dugouts had to be large enough to carry many warriors.

Colonists Use Water

When the colonists came, they used water just as the Indians did. They, too, used the waters for transportation.

The colonists built their settlements and plantations by rivers. They wanted to live in places they could get to easily. These places were on the banks of rivers and streams. The colonists traveled in dugouts from one place to another. The wide, slow rivers and streams of the Low Country were good roads.

Harbors

Our earliest cities grew up where Low Country rivers met the Atlantic Ocean. These

places became centers of trade. Planters brought their goods downstream by dugout. Then they put the goods on ships and sent them to buyers in Europe.

South Carolina has three natural **harbors.** A harbor is an area of water where large ships can come in and **dock** at the land. Our harbors are at Charleston and Georgetown and in Port Royal Sound near Beaufort.

A harbor for big, ocean-going ships has to have four things. First, it must have a good climate and good weather. It must also have an

easy way for ships to enter. It needs deep water. (The water must be deep enough for the ships at low tide.) And a harbor needs shelter from rough seas and high winds. Our South Carolina harbors have all four of these things.

Charleston, Georgetown, and Port Royal are South Carolina's three **ports.** A port is a city or town which has a harbor used for trade.

The Port of Charleston Today

The port of Charleston is still important for our trade with the rest of the world. Have you ever taken a tour of the harbor? Look at the pictures while you listen to the story.

READ TO ME

You are flying over Charleston harbor in a helicopter. You see some boats and ships coming into port. Others are going out.

One ship you see is a **freighter.** It is carrying goods from South America into Charleston. What do you think might be on the ship?

You see along the shore several areas where large ships are docked. These are called **terminals.** Here the **cargoes,** or shipments of goods, are loaded and unloaded.

The ships you see at one terminal look different from the freighter. They are **container ships.** The cargo for these ships is packed in large containers. The containers make cargo easy to store and to move.

You see many containers standing in a storage area at the terminal. Many of these containers will be loaded on the ships. You can see the large **cranes** that will be used to pick up and move the containers. Some of the containers will go inside the ship. Others will be placed on the ship's deck.

If you were down on the ground, you could see the size of the containers. They are about the size of a railroad boxcar. When a container is unloaded at the port, it can be placed on a railroad flat car or on a flatbed truck.

The train or truck will carry it to its final destination.

You can tell from the movement of ships and people in the harbor that it is a busy place. Over 3 1/2 million tons of cargo pass through the port each year. You can see why it is important to our state.

Up Country Water Travel

Water transportation helped make the Low Country rich from trade. It also helped settlers move into the Midlands. They moved upstream as far as they could travel. Where they had to stop, they built towns. Why do you think the settlers could travel no farther by boat?

The rapids, shoals, and waterfalls in the Up Country made water travel hard. People in the Up Country had trouble getting their goods to a port. They did not become rich from trade the way many Low Country people did.

After South Carolina became a state, Up Country people wanted better transportation. They began to build **canals.** Canals are man-made waterways. South Carolinians built canals to help boats get around shoals, rapids, and waterfalls. You can see remains of some of these canals today. Are there any near you?

The canals never worked as well as Up Country people hoped they would. Other forms of transportation became more important. You will learn more about them later.

Intracoastal Waterway

Canals were not very successful. But another man-made waterway has done well. This is the Intracoastal Waterway. It connects our river systems. The Waterway is made up of rivers, bays, and inlets joined by canals.

Perhaps you have driven on a bridge over the waterway. Some of the bridges are **drawbridges.** When a tall boat needs to go through, the sides of the bridge are raised. All cars have to stop using the bridge until the boat has gone through.

Early Water Power

Did you know that water could be used for power? The colonists used water power. They used it to run mills. At **grist mills** they ground grain into **meal,** a coarse flour. The power for these early mills came from a **waterwheel**.

Each mill was built by a moving stream, often at a waterfall. There was a huge wheel on the stream side of the mill. The water from the stream or waterfall turned the wheel. The turning wheel worked the machines inside the mill.

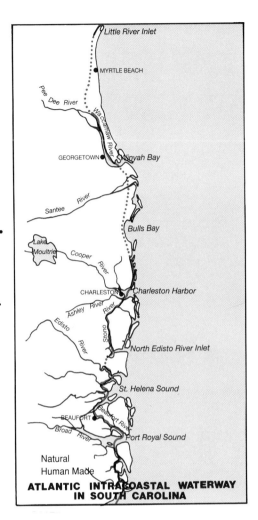

ATLANTIC INTRACOASTAL WATERWAY IN SOUTH CAROLINA

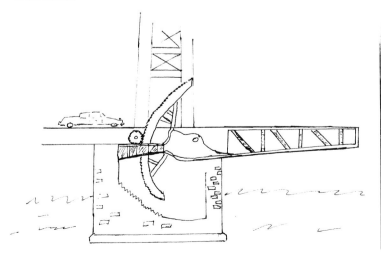

Water Power Today

South Carolinians still use water power. Today we have large **dams** which use water to make electricity. This kind of power is called **hydroelectric power.**

A dam is a wall built across a river. It keeps the water from flowing downstream. A gate in the dam can be opened to let some water through. The water running through the gate moves parts of a **generator.** The generator turns the water power into electricity.

Some power plants use water in the form of steam. The steam moves the parts of the generator to make electricity.

South Carolinians have built dams on many of our rivers. Each dam has made a lake. Look at the map of South Carolina. What lakes do you see? All of these lakes were made by dams.

LAKE JOGASSEE
LAKE KEOWEE
HARTWELL RESERVOIR
LAKE WYLIE
LAKE GREENWOOD
LAKE ROBINSON
LAKE WATEREE
CLARK HILL RESERVOIR
LAKE MURRAY
LAKE MARION
LAKE MOULTRIE
ATLANTIC OCEAN

DO YOU KNOW

When people build a dam, they know that a lake will form behind it. The river water will collect and cover large amounts of land behind the dam. What do people lose when a dam is built? What do they get?

Other Uses of Water

South Carolinians use their man-made lakes in many ways. For example, they use them as **reservoirs**. Reservoirs are large pools for storing water. People use reservoir water to drink and wash. They also use it to water crops. The reservoirs store water so South Carolinians have it when they need it.

South Carolinians also use the lakes for **recreation,** or fun. Have you ever gone to a lake for boating, water-skiing, or swimming?

Many South Carolinians enjoy fishing in our lakes. Among the fish they like to catch and eat

are perch, bream, catfish, and striped bass. The **striped bass** is South Carolina's state fish.

Some South Carolinians earn their living by raising fish for others to catch. These people work at fish **hatcheries.** Here fish are raised from eggs. When the fish are big enough, they are placed in our lakes and streams.

To some South Carolinians fishing is a sport and recreation. To others it is a way of making a living. Fishing is an important job, especially along the coast. It takes many South Carolinians to catch the fish, shellfish, and crabs people like to eat.

DO YOU KNOW

In Colleton County South Carolinians have started raising shrimp and other sea animals. This is called **mariculture,** or raising things in sea water. How do you think mariculture might help our state?

Water has always been an important resource for South Carolinians. They have used water for transportation and trade, for power, and for recreation. They have used the water to wash and to drink. And some have depended on water to make a living.

What would happen if South Carolina's water were not fit to drink? What if fish could no longer live in our waters or along our coast? Why is clean water important in our state?

In colonial times our harbors shipped many goods. These goods brought **pirates** to our coast. Pirates are the robbers of the sea.

One pirate was Edward Teach, called Blackbeard. He once stopped all ships going in and out of Charles Town harbor.

Anne Bonney was a Charles Town woman who married a pirate. She became one herself. When their ship was captured, her husband hid. But Anne fought until she was defeated.

· Colonists lost many goods to the pirates. But at last they got these robbers out of our coastal waters.

A CLOSER LOOK
SOUTH
CAROLINA
PIRATES

CHAPTER
13
LAND RESOURCES

Look around your classroom. What do you see? Look at the people in your room. What are they wearing? Now think about your home. What is it made of? Think about what you will eat for supper tonight. Where does that food come from?

All of the things you have seen and thought about come from the land. Many may have come from land in South Carolina. This chapter tells about how South Carolinians have used their land resources.

Early Land Use

South Carolinians have used the land to meet their basic needs. Think about the First South Carolinians. Think about their food, homes, and clothing. How did these come from the land?

The Indians also used the land to make their lives easier and better. Think about their tools, pots, and dishes. How did these come from the land?

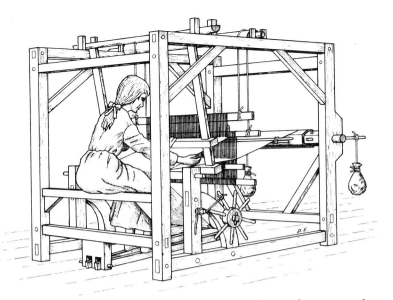

DO YOU KNOW

You can make dyes like people did in colonial times. Some everyday things like onion skins make good dyes. What other things will make dyes?

The Indians made their trading dugouts from trees. They caught animals for furs and skins. All these things came from the land.

The European settlers used the land to meet their needs, too. They grew vegetables and raised hogs and cattle.

For clothing they raised sheep and grew some cotton. The women spun the wool and cotton into yarn. Then they wove the yarn into cloth. To put color in their clothing, they used dyes. They made the dyes from plants.

To build their homes, the settlers used trees and clay they found here. Some learned to make clay into bricks. They used the bricks for houses and other buildings.

Most of the earliest settlers grew and found on the land all they needed to meet their needs. Soon some settlers began to **specialize.** These settlers produced more of something than they needed. Then they traded their product for things they did not produce.

Business in Animals

For many early settlers, using the land to raise animals became an important business. They could sell their pork and beef to people who lived on islands in the Caribbean Sea. In turn, they could buy products like sugar which they did not grow here.

Soon the colonists were raising large herds of cattle. They kept them in fenced areas called **cowpens.** Often slaves were put in charge of the cowpens. Some say these slaves were the first cowboys in the United States.

Some South Carolinians still use the land to raise animals. Many grassy fields of the

Piedmont are **pastures** where cattle graze. Farmers raise some of the cattle for food. They raise other cattle for **dairy** products like the milk you drink.

Farmers also still raise hogs for food. Have you eaten pork **barbeque?** The idea for barbeque came from the Indians. They cooked large pieces of meat over a fire. Have you ever been to a barbeque and seen meat cooking over a fire?

When the colonists came, they began to raise horses. They rode horses and used them to pull wagons and carriages. Today South Carolinians race them, show them, and use them for recreation.

South Carolinians also raise **poultry**— chickens and turkeys. They raise both for meat. And they also raise chickens for their eggs.

DO YOU KNOW ?

South Carolina has more peach **orchards** than Georgia. (And Georgia calls itself the "peach state"!) Only one state has more peach orchards than South Carolina. It is in the western part of the United States. What state do you think it is?

Business in Food Plants

Some colonists produced more meat than they needed. Others grew more **grain** and vegetables than they could use. Sometimes they sold the grain so it could be made into flour or meal for bread. Sometimes they sold the grain as feed for cattle and other animals. The colonists sold their extra vegetables, too.

Today many farmers continue to grow plants which produce food for people and animals. Some South Carolinians are **truck farmers.** They raise vegetables to sell.

Fruit Farming

Long ago people in the Up Country and the Midlands found that peaches and apples grew well there. Some people grew enough apples and peaches that they could sell them to others. South Carolina still has a large fresh fruit crop for sale each year.

Soybeans

One of our newest money crops is **soybeans.** People started planting soybeans to feed cattle and to improve the soil.

Today people use soybeans in many ways. They use some of them to make oil, meal, and flour. Soybean oil is used for margarine, in paint, and in soap. Soy meal is used to feed farm animals. Soy flour is used in bread, puddings, and many other foods. Because soybeans have so many uses, many people want to buy part of our crop.

Fairs

Each year farmers like to get together to show what they have raised on the land. These get-togethers are called **fairs.** At a fair prizes are given for the best animals, vegetables, pickles, and so on.

**People
Places
Things**

The South Carolina State Fair is held in Columbia each fall. Why is that a good time of year for it?

You can learn a lot about our use of land from a fair. Is there one near you?

Tobacco Farming

Some South Carolina farmers raise and sell tobacco. Many years ago tobacco became an important crop in the Pee Dee area. Tobacco grows well in the sandy soil of the coastal plain. It has grown so well that today it is one of South Carolina's money crops.

Do you know how tobacco was grown years ago? Look at the pictures as you listen to the story.

READ TO ME

Marion County, 1950

My name is Henry Parker. I'm a tobacco farmer. Growing tobacco is hard work. Most of it we do by hand. First we plant the tiny seeds in special seed beds. When the seeds have grown just enough, we move the small plants to the fields.

As the plants grow, we have to tend them carefully. When the bottom leaves turn yellow, we pick the tobacco leaves by hand. We take the leaves to a square, wooden barn. There we tie the leaves onto sticks and hang them in the barn.

We burn a wood stove in the barn to **cure** the tobacco. Curing changes the color of the leaves and dries them. We have to make sure the temperature in the barn is just right. Someone has to watch the curing 24 hours a day to be sure everything is going well. The curing takes three to five days.

When the tobacco is cured, we can sell it. Tobacco is sold at an **auction,** a special sale where buyers **bid** for it. The tobacco goes to the one who makes the highest bid.

I take my tobacco to a warehouse in Mullins. There it is sorted and auctioned. If you came to a tobacco auction, you would not be able to understand what people were saying. There is a lot of noise. The **auctioneer** talks very fast, and the buyers use signals to make their bids. Can you imagine 200 pounds of tobacco sold by the lift of an eyebrow?

Today there are machines to pick the tobacco. There are also big curing barns which keep the heat just right. Growing tobacco is not done by hand as much any more.

Farming Problems

South Carolina farmers sometimes face problems. Some problems are caused by weather. For example, peach growers watch the temperature carefully in spring. Very cold temperatures can hurt the peach buds.

Another weather problem is **drought.** A drought is a long period when there is no rain. Farmers can lose their crops.

Today some farmers are using **irrigation** to keep their fields moist during a drought. They often use reservoir water to irrigate the fields.

Another problem is stopping erosion. Sometimes heavy rains wash good soil out of the fields.

Cotton farming has shown other problems farmers face. One big problem is keeping the land fertile. What happens to the land when cotton is planted year after year?

People Places Things →

Kudzu

Kudzu is a vine from Asia. People found it could stop erosion. They began to plant it in eroded cotton fields. The kudzu grew quickly. It covered the ground. But it also grew up into trees, up telephone poles, and over old buildings. Have you seen kudzu growing where you live?

Insects are another problem for farmers. An insect made it hard to grow cotton. The insect is the **boll weevil.** The boll weevil loves cotton bolls. It eats the cotton plant. And it destroys bolls by laying eggs in them.

When it first came here, the boll weevil ruined much of our cotton crop. Cotton farmers still have to watch out for the weevil.

What other insects cause problems for farmers?

Business In Forests

Forestry is an important business in our state. It has been important since colonial times. Do you remember ways the settlers used the trees?

South Carolina wood and wood products were used by early ship builders. The tall pine made fine masts for sailing ships. Ship builders liked to use live oak for their ships. The wood could stand the pounding of the sea for many years.

Today we use our trees mainly for lumber, or boards, and for making paper. Trees are cut into lumber at large sawmills all over the state. Some wood goes to paper mills.

Because trees are so important to the state, as people cut down some trees, they plant new ones. This is a good way to save our forest resources.

The Adventure

Use Of Minerals

Agriculture and forestry have been the two most important uses of land in South Carolina. But the land has also provided some minerals for our use.

Settlers in the Up Country found iron there. They mined the **ore.** (The ore is the mineral mixed with dirt and rock.) Then they heated it to separate the metal from the rock. They used the iron to make tools, fences, horseshoes, and weapons. South Carolinians stopped mining iron when they could buy better iron for less money from other Americans.

Did you know there is gold in South Carolina? It is in seven counties above the fall line. Gold was first mined here about 150 years ago. At one time the Haile Gold Mine in Lancaster County

produced more gold than any other mine in the eastern United States.

Much of South Carolina's soil is clay. One special clay is called **kaolin.** Kaolin is mined and made into fine pottery. It is also used for bathtubs. And it makes the shiny surface you see on magazine paper.

Granite is another mineral found here. It is dug out of open pits called **quarries.** The best known quarries are near Winnsboro. They produce **blue granite** which is our state stone. Granite is used in roads, statues, gravestones, and buildings. The walls and columns of the State House are made of South Carolina granite.

Vermiculite, sand, and limestone are also found here. Vermiculite is used to keep things hot or cool. Sand from the Sand Hills is important for making glass. Our limestone makes good cement.

The land has always been important to South Carolinians. They have used it to grow crops and animals. They have used it to grow trees for building and for paper. They have used the minerals in the land to make roads, buildings, tools and other products.

South Carolinians have used the land

to live and to make a living. **How are our ways of using the land today the same as the early settlers' ways? How are they different? What lessons have we learned about taking care of the land?**

Some of South Carolina's gold is deep in rock. It has to be mined. There is another kind of gold here, too. This is called **placer** (PLAH-ser) gold. Small bits of it can be found in sand and gravel which have eroded from rock.

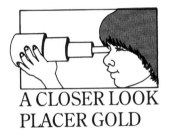

A CLOSER LOOK
PLACER GOLD

To find this gold, people go to an Up Country stream. They look for a sandbar or a large rock where eroded sand and gravel collect. They shovel some of the sand and gravel into a pan. They use the stream water to wash all the small pieces out of the pan. Then they use tweezers to sort through the big pieces and pick out any gold. They put the gold in a small bottle.

CHAPTER
14
HUMAN RESOURCES

Did you know that you are a resource? All South Carolinians are. All people are **human resources.** People can do work. They can produce or make goods to sell. People can perform **services,** do helpful things for other people. People can be **creative.** They can find new and better ways of doing things.

South Carolina has grown because of the goods, services, and ideas which have come from people. This chapter is about how human resources have helped our state grow.

Human Resources in Agriculture

Human resources made "King Cotton" possible. People planted the cotton, tended it, and picked it. They **experimented** with, or tried, different kinds of cotton seed. They found kinds of cotton which would grow all over the state. They found kinds the boll weevil did not like.

Developing better seeds and new **varieties,** or kinds, of plants takes time and work. Many South Carolinians do this for a living.

Coker Farms

Robert R. Coker of Hartsville set up farms to develop better varieties of seeds and plants. Coker was a leader in finding ways to improve agriculture in South Carolina. New seeds and new ways of farming spread from the Coker farms all over the world.

People Places Things

Man checks cotton on Coker Farms

People have also found better ways to use what they grow. When South Carolinians first grew cotton, they used just the fiber. They threw most of the seeds away.

Then somebody thought the seeds could be used for something. People built cottonseed mills. There they pressed the seeds to get oil. They made the rest of the seed into meal.

People have improved agriculture in another way. They have **invented** and built machines to do some of the work they once did. What machines have made farming easier?

Industry

Machines make work easier for people. Machines can help make more goods faster. That's why people like them.

The early settlers had simple machines to help them do their work. These machines used muscle power or human energy. For example, women used a spinning wheel and a loom to make yarn and cloth. They used their hands and feet to make the machines move.

Later South Carolinians heard that yarn and cloth could be made in water-powered mills. So people began building cotton mills. Since that time, the textile industry has been important here.

People have set up many other industries in South Carolina. Today South Carolina has paper mills and glass factories. It has factories which make aluminum and ones which make tires. It has some which make machinery and some which make computer parts. What industries are near your home?

Some of our industries have been brought here by people from other countries. People from Germany, Switzerland, France, Japan, and Great Britain have built factories here. They have helped our state grow.

Roads

Both agriculture and industry produce goods. These goods have to be sold for people to make money. To sell their goods, people have to get them to market. They need good transportation.

In the Low Country, water provided good transportation. Up Country people had to travel

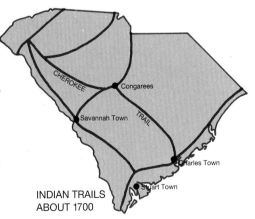

INDIAN TRAILS
ABOUT 1700

Foster's Tavern

over land. At first there were no roads. Traders had to follow Indian paths. When South Carolinians began to build roads, they built them on these paths.

The early roads were not **paved** like ours are today. Some were just dirt paths. Some were topped with a layer of sand and gravel. Others had a layer of crushed shells on top. People walked, rode horses, and drove wagons on the roads. They also herded animals down the roads. Sometimes they rode in carriages or **stagecoaches.**

The stagecoaches carried passengers from one place to another. Sometimes the trips were long. Passengers had to spend the night in an **inn** or hotel. Where there was no inn, they stayed in a home that took guests.

There was a big problem with travel by land in the early days. How were people to cross a deep, swift stream or river?

Where the stream was wide, men provided a ferry service. The ferryman owned a large flat boat called a **ferry.** He took travelers, their horses, and wagons across the stream. People paid to use the ferry.

DO YOU KNOW You can tell where some of the old ferries were by looking at place names. Can you find Galivants Ferry in Horry County? Do you know Garner's Ferry Road in Columbia?

Where the stream was narrow, people built bridges. The first bridges were short. They could be no longer than the height of a tree. Do you know why? Later on people found that bridges would last longer if they were covered. They built roofs over them.

Just as people had to pay for the ferry, they had to pay to cross a bridge. The amount they paid was called a **toll.**

Railroads

Human resources have brought better transportation to our state. The roads helped people get their goods to market. The canals helped, too. Then some people in Charleston had an even better idea. They would bring the railroad to South Carolina.

Would you like to know what that first railroad was like? Follow the pictures as you listen to the story.

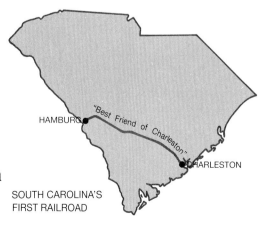

HAMBURG
"Best Friend of Charleston"
CHARLESTON

SOUTH CAROLINA'S
FIRST RAILROAD

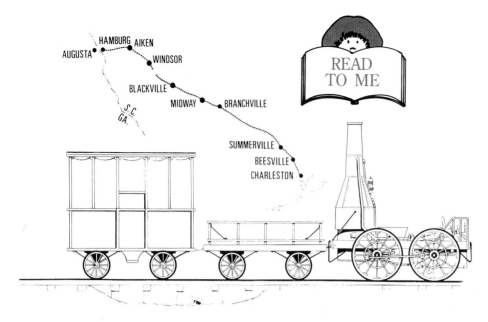

each stop. Every time the train stopped, the soldiers fired the cannon. Everyone celebrated the coming of the railroad.

Well, not everyone. The company did have trouble getting permission to lay track. Some people didn't like the noise of the whistles and bells. Some farmers were afraid their animals would wander onto the track and be hurt. Finally a law was passed that said the railroad had to have a person ride in front of the engine to look out for animals. Some railroads put a statue of a boy holding a flag on the **cowcatcher** instead.

The Best Friend was a great train. Unfortunately, it did not last long. A fireman got tired of the hissing sound of the steam. When he tried to stop it, the engine exploded. But other locomotives took *The Best Friend's* place. Railroads began to spread out over the state.

Charleston, 1835

My name is James McDavid. My friend, E.L. Miller, designed the first locomotive for the first railroad in South Carolina. The locomotive was called "The Best Friend of Charleston." What a fine train that was! It ran on steam power. The car behind the engine carried wood. A fireman put wood in the fire in the boiler. The boiler heated water to make steam. The steam made the locomotive go.

The Best Friend pulled passenger cars and freight cars. The passenger cars were open carriages. At first some people were afraid to ride the trains. They did not like the ashes and sparks that sometimes blew onto them from the smokestack on the engine.

I remember the first trip of *The Best Friend*. The first six miles of track were open. The train carried 141 passengers. It went 25 miles an hour! A few months later *The Best Friend* made a special trip. It carried some United States soldiers and a cannon. Young girls spread flowers on the track to welcome *The Best Friend* to

The railroad was a big success in South Carolina. Many miles of track were built. The railroads finally gave the Up Country good transportation.

Branchville

A place where two lines of track cross is called a **junction.** The first railroad junction in the United States was in South Carolina. The builders of our first railroad decided to add a branch that would go to Columbia. The branch formed the first railroad junction. A town called Branchville grew up there. At the museum in Branchville you can learn about our early railroads.

People Places Things

Automobiles And Airplanes

There were no cars in South Carolina until 1900. The first one appeared in Columbia that year. South Carolinians didn't take to cars right away. Many thought they were a **fad** and wouldn't last. Others thought the roads were too bad and cars cost too much.

But in the next 25 years some people did buy cars. In Columbia there were enough cars to have accidents. Columbia had to put in a traffic light. It was the first stop light in the state. Soon many other cities and towns had them, too.

Some people in South Carolina even built cars. The Anderson Motor Car Company in

Rock Hill built cars and small trucks. Anderson cars were good, but they cost a lot. The company went out of business.

The more cars people had, the more they knew they needed better roads. So they began to pave highways. They called these "all-weather roads."

Better roads meant that more people bought cars. Farmers and industry began to use trucks. And then people decided to bring buses into South Carolina to carry passengers.

When the airplane was invented, South Carolinians decided they wanted air transportation, too. They built airports and began to use planes for air mail, freight, and passengers.

Today automobile, truck, and airplane are the main forms of transportation in the state. But people still use railroads and boats, too. These forms of transportation make it possible for South Carolinians to get their goods to market. They help South Carolinians travel more and farther. Human resources made these things possible.

Tourists

Some South Carolinians saw that people were traveling more. They decided to provide places where **tourists,** travelers, could go for recreation. Myrtle Beach grew this way. One man built a hotel. Many people came to enjoy the beach and stay in his hotel. Other people built other hotels. Still others added golf courses, water slides, museums, and other things for tourists to see and do. Entertaining tourists is an important business in South Carolina.

Services For People

People take care of their water resources. They take care of their land resources. But how do they take care of their human resources?

First, they try to keep people healthy. South Carolina has doctors and hospitals to keep South Carolinians well. And there are medical schools to train new doctors.

People
Places
Things

Lucy Hughes Brown

Many years ago only men became doctors. Dr. Lucy Hughes Brown was the first woman doctor in Charleston. She was the first black woman doctor in our state. South Carolina has both men and women doctors now.

Second, they help people learn what they need to know to be good workers and come up with good ideas.

South Carolina provides schools for all children. In the state there are many colleges, too. Some of these colleges train teachers.

Winthrop College

Winthrop College in Rock Hill was started to train women to be teachers. The college was "Pitchfork Ben" Tillman's idea. Both men and women now go to Winthrop.

People Places Things

South Carolinians have made our state what it is today. They have decided how to use our natural resources and how to take care of them.

How do you think South Carolina would be different if people had not brought the railroad here? How would it be different if they hadn't built mills and started other industries?

You are one of South Carolina's human resources. Are you learning what you will need to know? What would you like to do to help our state grow?

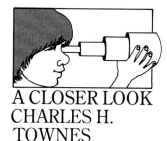

A CLOSER LOOK
CHARLES H.
TOWNES

Scientists are important human resources. One South Carolinian won the Nobel Prize for his work in science. Charles Townes grew up in Greenville. He was a top science student. He taught science all over the world.

One morning Dr. Townes sat on a park bench in Washington, D.C. He added up numbers on the back of an envelope. The numbers gave him the key to a great invention called the maser. The maser made possible a clock that keeps almost perfect time.

The maser led to another invention, the laser. The laser lets people use light in new ways. A laser beam can cut hard objects. It can be used in medicine. No wonder Charles Townes is in the South Carolina Hall of Fame.

Reviewing Main Ideas

1. How have South Carolinians used natural resources to make a living?
2. How has our use of land resources changed? How has our use of water resources changed?
3. What are human resources? How have human resources helped South Carolina grow?
4. Why do we need to conserve and protect our resources?
5. What are some ways we can protect our resources?

Using New Vocabulary

Think about the new words below. Arrange them in two or three groups so that each word fits in only one group. Name the groups. Be ready to explain your work.

waterwheel	tobacco	canal
drawbridge	granite	kaolin
peach orchard	soybeans	ore
placer gold	reservoir	harbor

Can you think of other words that can go in your groups?

Remembering People and Places

Tell why we should remember each of these:

Charleston harbor
Best Friend of Charleston
Intercoastal Waterway
Branchville

If you could add one person or place to this list, what would you add? Why?

Thinking About South Carolina

1. What problems would South Carolina have if we did not have a good water supply? good harbors?
2. How would business in South Carolina be different if we did not have fertile land? good forests? minerals?
3. What special ability or talent makes you a resource? What can you do to develop your talent?
4. Human resources often have to solve problems. Pick a problem in your community or school. How do you think the problem can be solved? Why?

Being Creative

Humans are creative and often invent important machines. Draw and describe a machine that you might invent to solve a natural or human resource problem in our state.

HERITAGE

You have learned about our environment, our history, and our ways of living. These have been passed on to us by earlier South Carolinians. These are our **heritage.**

In this unit you will learn more about your heritage. You will learn how people **preserve,** or save, their heritage. You will learn how they pass it on to their children. You will learn about your family heritage. And you will learn about your community and state heritage.

In this unit you will learn that:

1. Knowing about the past helps us understand who we are.
2. Our families do many things to preserve their heritage.
3. Our rich heritage comes from the people who have come to and lived in our state.
4. The communities we live in are a part of our heritage.
5. Communities and other groups of South Carolinians help to preserve our heritage.
6. Conserving our environment helps to keep our state a good place to live and work.

CHAPTER
15
FAMILY HERITAGE

Part of our heritage comes from people who came before us in our families. Each of our families has a history. We are part of that history. Each of our families has **customs,** or special ways of doing things. We learn those customs from our families.

In this chapter you will learn about some of the customs of South Carolina families. You will learn how our families pass on their customs to the children.

Family History

Today all kinds of people live in South Carolina. Some are Native Americans. Their **ancestors** (earlier family members) were the First South Carolinians. Other people have ancestors from Europe, Africa, Asia, and other parts of the world. Who were your ancestors? From what part of the world did they come?

Some of our families have lived in South Carolina for many years. Other families have just moved here. How long has your family been in our state? Where else has your family lived?

Where the family comes from is a part of the family's history. So are the places where the family has lived. So are the names of family members today and long ago. Knowing their family history helps people understand who they are.

Many families keep **records** of the history of their family. They write down names of ancestors and information about them. They keep information about present-day family members, too.

Some families keep their records in the family Bible. Often this Bible is passed down from one **generation** to another.

A generation is a time in family history. You live in one generation. Your parents are in another. Your grandparents are in still another generation.

DO YOU KNOW?

You have thousands of ancestors. Count back ten generations. (That is back to about the time South Carolina was settled.) Start with you as one. Your parents are two more. Your grandparents are 4 more. Your great-grandparents are 8 more. That's four generations back. **Six more steps back and you have a total of 2,042 ancestors!**

Many families preserve their history by saving things that belonged to their ancestors. Sometimes the family still uses these things. Sometimes they store the things carefully.

Your family may have old family pictures or an old photo **album.** They may have diaries written by your ancestors. Or they may have old **scrapbooks.** They may have trunks full of old clothes and letters.

Does your family keep any of these things? You can learn a lot about your heritage from these objects.

Sometimes families have **reunions.** At a reunion, family members from all over the state and country get together. Reunions are ways families use to preserve their heritage.

1958 GRAMLING REUNION
WHITE HOUSE METHODIST CHURCH
ORANGEBURG, SOUTH CAROLINA

At reunions people tell old family stories. These stories may begin, "Do you remember the time . . .?" Families remember their history by telling these stories.

People may also tell new stories about family members at a reunion. These new stories will be retold at later reunions. They will become a part of the family history.

Family Customs

Many of the things we do today we learned from our ancestors. When we do things the old ways, we remember who we are and where we came from. And we pass this heritage on to our children.

Language

Some South Carolinians still speak the language of their ancestors. They speak English, but they also know the old language. Does your family speak Greek, Italian, Chinese, or another language? Do you know a family that does?

**People
Places
Things**

Gullah

Gullah is a special language in our state. It comes from both African speech and English the way it was spoken long ago. It was the language blacks and whites spoke to each other on the Low Country plantations.

Gullah has been preserved by some families in parts of the Low Country.

Here's an old Gullah saying. "Ef yo' ent hab hoss to ride, ride cow." What do you think it means?

Food

Most South Carolinians eat foods prepared as their ancestors prepared them. They may use a **recipe** that came from mother or grandmother or great-grandmother.

Perhaps you eat pilau (PUHR-LOE). Families made this rice-and-meat dish after the Civil War when food was hard to get. Many families still enjoy it.

Do you eat red rice or Hoppin' John? Do you eat okra and cornbread? Do you eat chitterlings (CHIT-linz)? If you do, the recipes may have been passed down in your family.

As new families have come to our state, they have brought new recipes with them. Have you ever eaten lasagna? Italian families brought that recipe. Greek families brought souvlaki. Chinese families brought moo goo gai pan.

Families from all other the world have brought their eating customs to our state. Many have set up restaurants where they serve family dishes to other South Carolinians.

Crafts

Many families preserve the **crafts** of their ancestors. A craft is a skill in making something by hand.

Some South Carolinians still make things the way their ancestors did. Have you seen any sweet grass baskets? They are made by many Low Country women. These women weave sweet grass, pine straw, and split palm into beautiful basket shapes.

Have you ever slept in a hammock? Some Low Country people still make hammocks the old way, by hand.

Many people in the Up Country preserve old mountain crafts. Some make **quilts.** Quilts are bed coverings. They were used like blankets are used today. A young girl began making quilts as soon as she could sew. She would need many quilts for the new family she would have when she married.

Women made quilts out of colorful pieces of

cloth. They sewed cloth pieces together to make designs. Quilt designs were passed on from generation to generation. Some families make these quilts the same way today.

Stories

Some South Carolinians are **storytellers.** They pass on stories told by our ancestors. And they tell the stories the way our ancestors told them.

Some tell stories passed down by blacks. Stories about Br'er Rabbit, Br'er Fox, and Br'er Bear are part of our heritage.

Others tell old Cherokee tales. Still others tell mountain stories and ghost stories.

Look in your library for books of Carolina stories. Perhaps you can learn to tell one yourself.

Music and Dance

People also preserve the dances and music of their ancestors. Can you do the Charleston? This dance started many years ago in South Carolina. Our ancestors have passed it on to us. Can you clog? Many mountain families preserve this old dance.

Can you do the shag? Your parents or grandparents may be able to teach you. This dance was once done to **beach music.** It was popular in the 1960s. Many people still dance the shag and enjoy beach music.

Another kind of music our ancestors enjoyed was **jazz.** Many South Carolinians still enjoy it. They may have learned about jazz from their parents. They may have heard a great jazz musician like Dizzy Gillespie.

John Birks (Dizzy) Gillespie is from Cheraw. He learned to play the trumpet and started playing jazz. Jazz was a new kind of music that started in the South. Gillespie has written jazz and played his music all over the world. He has helped preserve jazz for generations to come.

What kinds of music and dancing do you like? Will you teach these to your children?

Two Families

Often we can learn about our heritage by talking with our families. Do you ask your parents what life was like when they were your age? Do you ask your grandparents? Does your family have special stories members retell when they get together? Does your family keep photo albums and scrapbooks?

Listen to two young South Carolinians who have learned about their family heritage.

READ TO ME

Columbia

My name is Helen Elizabeth, but everyone calls me Beth. I was named for my grandmothers. I was born in Columbia and have never lived anywhere else.

My father was born in St. Louis, Missouri. His family moved to South Carolina. Granddad was really coming back home. He grew up in Branchville where his father was the town's doctor. Daddy has lived in many different places, but he says he likes South Carolina best of all.

My mother was born in Columbia. Her family has lived in South Carolina for a long, long time. She likes being a South Carolinian and so do I.

Momma tells stories about when she was growing up in Columbia. She even takes my sister Katie and me to places she remembers from her childhood. Columbia has changed since she was a little girl. My grandmother also grew up in Columbia. Her stories are about an earlier time. Some day I will tell stories about Columbia, too.

Both Momma and my grandmother tell about their first grade teacher. The same teacher taught them. Both of them remember that teacher as their favorite teacher. I wonder who I will remember as my favorite teacher.

My great-grandfather's stories are the best of all. He grew up on a farm in Saluda County. When he was a boy, there were no cars, planes, televisions, or anything electrical. He said that he had to walk or ride a mule five miles to school.

One day I'll wear the ring and pearls that Granddad gave Grandmother and Daddy gave Momma. I'll have the Indian tomahawk my great-grandpa found in Saluda County when he was a boy. I'll have the glass cup and saucer that was given to my great-great-grandmother in 1901. (It has the name Elizabeth on it.) These things will have a special place in my home.

The stories and the things we have from the past help me know about my family's heritage. They will help me remember it when I grow up. When I have a family, I sure will have lots of stories to tell.

Spartanburg

My name is Robb. My family moved to Spartanburg when I was three. We lived in Baltimore, Maryland before we came here. We moved here when my father got a new job. We are the only members of our family who live in South Carolina. We have relatives in Tennessee, Kentucky, Virginia, and Pennsylvania.

We like to get together with our relatives whenever we can. Sometimes my father's family vacations with us at the beach. The best times are when my uncles and aunts come along with my grandpar-

ents. Everybody talks about the old days when they were growing up together.

One favorite story always comes up. That's the one about how Uncle John burned down the shed and my dad got punished for it. Another favorite story is about how my dad won a championship football game in the last 6 seconds.

We have pictures of Dad's teammates carrying him off the field after the game. They had him up on their shoulders. The picture was printed in the newspaper, and Grandma Emilie cut it out. She put that and many other things into a scrapbook for Dad and Uncle John. She has taken many family pictures and put them in photo albums.

Sometimes we visit my mother's mother in Pennsylvania. She lives in an old house that has been in the family for a hundred years. The house has many things my ancestors used. The furniture in the living room belonged to my great-great-aunts. So did the dishes we use for special dinners. My great-great-aunts made the quilts my grandmother has on the beds. This grandmother has boxes of old letters and clothes in her attic. They're fun to look at.

Some of the things in my home in Spartanburg came from my grandmother's house. Our dining room table came from there. One of the family quilts is on my bed.

Even though I don't see the rest of our family very often, when I look around the house I see reminders of them. I often think of the stories about my parents when they were young. I wonder what stories I will pass on to my children when they grow up.

Children learn customs by doing things the way their families do them. They listen to older family members share favorite stories and music. They watch older family members dance and make things.

South Carolina has a rich heritage of customs from all over the world. When we use some of our family customs, we understand a little better who we are. When we learn about the history and customs of our friends and neighbors, we can understand them better.

What parts of your heritage will you want to pass on to your children?

A CLOSER LOOK
WILLIAM
GILMORE SIMMS

As a child, William Gilmore Simms loved ghost stories. He also loved history, especially the history of our state. Simms became a fine storyteller and a great writer. His life in Charleston was hard. He could not afford to go to the best school. But he read everything he could find.

When he was about your age, he wrote poems about the War of 1812. His father had fought in the war and told William wonderful tales about it.

William Gilmore Simms became a writer. Many of the things he wrote contained stories he heard from people he met.

Simms wrote a history of South Carolina for boys and girls. That was many years ago. What do you think he told about in his book?

CHAPTER
16
COMMUNITY HERITAGE

Your heritage comes partly from your family. It also comes from the place or places you have lived. Your heritage comes from your country, your state, and your community.

A community is a place. It is also a group of people. People who live and work together in an area form a community.

This chapter tells about South Carolina communities. You will learn how they help preserve our heritage.

Communities

Most people live in communities. They live in a place with other people. They decide to work together to make their area a good place to live.

Some communities are small. Others are large. Some cover only a small area of land. Others cover a large area. Look at the map. How does it show communities with a small area? How does it show communities with a large area?

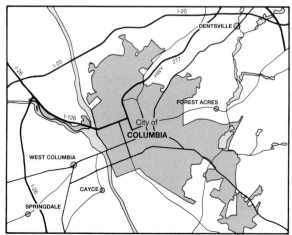

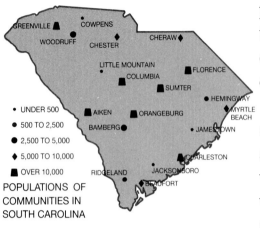

- • UNDER 500
- • 500 TO 2,500
- • 2,500 TO 5,000
- ♦ 5,000 TO 10,000
- ■ OVER 10,000

POPULATIONS OF
COMMUNITIES IN
SOUTH CAROLINA

Communities can also be small or large in **population.** The population of a community is the number of people who live there. How does the map show the population of each community?

Villages and towns have a small area and a small population. Cities have a large area and a large population. All communities are small when they begin. Charleston and Columbia were once small towns. Greenville began as a small town, too. Only about 500 people lived there when Andrew Jackson was President.

Towns

Towns start in places which attract people. People will live in places where they can make a living. Some South Carolina towns began at a **crossroads.** This is a place where two roads meet and cross. Traders and travelers use both roads.

Charleston flea market

The crossroads becomes a place where people can trade goods. Someone starts a store at the crossroads. Then someone else builds a hotel. People who work at the store and hotel build homes there. More people come and build homes. Towns that grew up at crossroads are trading centers.

Florence

Florence was named for a girl, Florence Harllee. She was the daughter of General W.W. Harllee of Marion. General Harllee built a railroad line. One station or **depot** on the line was named Florence after his daughter. The stagecoach also ran from this depot. A town grew around this depot at the crossroads of the railroad and the stage line. The town took its name from the depot.

People Places Things

People could earn money in a trading center. Many went there to live and work. They could make a living by working at a mill, too. Many South Carolina communities grew around mills—grist mills, sawmills, textile mills.

Towns also start at places chosen for government buildings. You already know that Columbia was planned as a center of our state government. Some of our communities began as centers of county government.

County Seats

A county is an area of our state. It has a government, just like our state does. Counties have a county **council** to make rules and decisions for the county. Counties also have courts.

Court House Square, Orangeburg, before paved roads

Each county needs a town for government buildings. It needs a town for the county courthouse. This town is called a **county seat.** That means it is where the county government sits. What is the county seat of your county?

Town Growth

All of our communities began as small towns. As more people moved to the town, the population grew. The people, or **citizens,** worked together to make their community a better place. Often the first thing they did together was build a church. Soon after that, they might build a school. Often the minister at the church also taught at the school.

As the town grew, it would get a post office. Someone would build a bank. Someone would open a restaurant. Many more stores would open. Someone would start a newspaper.

Winnsboro town clock

Fairfield County Courthouse

Newspapers

The first newspaperwoman in the United States was Elizabeth Timothy of Charleston. Before the Revolution, she ran the Carolina *Gazette.* The *Gazette* was the first newspaper in South Carolina.

The first newspaper in the Up Country was *Miller's Weekly Messenger.* It was printed in Pendleton by John Miller. You could get the paper for a year for $2.50.

**People
Places
Things**

Books by South Carolina writers are in your library. Try to find some by Peggy Parrish from Manning. Peggy Parrish went to USC. She became a third grade teacher. Later she became a writer for children. Have you read any of her stories about Amelia Bedelia? You will find them in your library.

As the town population grew, the town would need a government. Many towns elected a council. Often they elected a **mayor** to lead the town government. What is the government of your community like?

The town government needed a building. So the town would build a **town hall.** (It is called a city hall in a city.) Near the town hall the community would build a jail. All of these buildings were paid for with **taxes.**

The town government would also use the tax money to provide **services.** They would pay policemen and firemen to protect the town. They would build new streets.

As the town grew larger, new buildings would appear. There might be a hospital, a theatre, a library.

Kinds of Communities

Our largest communities are cities. A city has a large population. It covers a large area. Many people who work in our cities live in **suburbs.** Suburbs are communities right outside the city. Suburbs have many houses. But they have fewer businesses and industries than a city. What kind of community do you live in? Do you live in a city, or **urban**, community? Do you live in a **suburban** community? Do you live in a small town or a **rural**, or farming, area?

Community Festivals

The kind of community you live in is a part of your heritage. The place where your community is located is part of your heritage. The things your community is known for are part of your heritage.

Each community has things that make it a special place. Communities are proud of the

Come See Me Festival, Rock Hill

Parade, Salley Chitlin' Strut

Magnolia Gardens

things that make them special. They are proud of the industries and businesses that have helped them grow. They are proud of what their citizens have done to help our state.

Many South Carolina communities have celebrations, called **festivals.** Some festivals remind us of dance, music, and theatre in our communities.

Other festivals remind us of how people in our communities earn a living.

Still other festivals remind us of the customs of citizens of the community.

And other festivals remind us of the beautiful flowers and gardens in our communities.

DO YOU KNOW

Two flowers were named for South Carolinians. The gardenia was named for Dr. Alexander Garden. He brought this white flower to Beaufort from Africa.

Joel Poinsett of Greenville brought a red flower from Mexico to our state. That flower is now called a poinsettia.

Community History

Every community has a history. Communities remember their past in many ways. Often the names of streets tell about the history of the community. In Greenville, for example, there is a road named Pleasantburg. Pleasantburg Village was the small community from which Greenville grew.

Look at the street names in your community. Do the names tell anything about your community history?

Communities keep a record of their past in many ways. The county courthouse has records about who owned land in each community. It has records which show when each building was built.

Newspapers keep records, too. They have old issues of the paper. And they keep old photographs.

Some communities have their own **museums.** The museum keeps things that were once used in the community. It shows people how their ancestors lived in the community.

Sometimes communities act out what life was like in the old days. They may act out a battle that was near the town, for example. Often they do this on the **anniversary** of the battle. (An anniversary is the same date in a later year.)

Many communities in South Carolina have preserved old buildings. You can see parts of our community heritage when you visit these places.

Battle at Ninety Six

Nancy Stevenson was the first woman Lieutenant Governor of South Carolina. She was a community leader before she was a state leader. She worked hard in Charleston to help preserve the historic part of the city.

St. Michael's Church, Charleston

Often citizens who are interested in community history belong to the Historical Society. This group studies community history. And it helps restore old buildings.

Historic Brattonsville before restoration (*left*), and after restoration (*right*).

An Old House

Have you wondered how an old house might be restored? Listen to the story.

Suppose there is an old house in your community. Suppose it was one of the first homes there. The Historical Society may want to preserve it. Perhaps the Society buys the house, or maybe the owner gives it to the Society. Then the fun begins.

Imagine the Society wants to restore the house. They want it to look the way it did when the first family lived in it. To do this, they have to study the history of the house. They check the courthouse records to find out when the house was built and who owned it at different times. They see if new parts were added to the house and who added them.

They read diaries and records kept by the first owners. They study **inventories** of the house. An inventory is a list. The inventory might name things that were in the house at one time.

They study the kinds of furniture people had then. They find out how people decorated their homes. They find out what the family would have had in each room of the house.

They may look around the house to see if they can find any things left from the first family's time. Present-day family members may have things passed down to them from the first family. They may give things to display in the restored house.

After a long period of study, work can begin on restoring the house. This work takes time and money. It takes special workmen who can make the house look as it did many years ago. But in the end the house is restored. It becomes a house museum. You can visit it to see how people lived in the early days of your community. How would you rather learn about your community—read about it or see a restored home?

Your community is a part of your heritage. People in your community have special customs. They have particular ways of making a living. Your community has a history. Your community's past is a part of your past.

Citizens in a community work together to make it a good place to live. They are proud of their community. They celebrate all the ways it is special. They help preserve its history.

What is special about your community? How could you remind other citizens about how your community is special?

Cemeteries, or graveyards, are important places for people to preserve. They help us remember the past.

You can learn a lot about the past from **tombstones** (gravestones). They can help you trace your family history. And they can tell interesting things about family life years ago.

Tombstones can also tell about your town or city. They can tell you who lived there. They can tell you which citizens fought in our wars. They can tell you how long people lived long ago.

Are there any old cemeteries in your community? They would be interesting to visit.

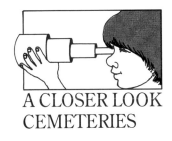

A CLOSER LOOK
CEMETERIES

CHAPTER 17

STATE HERITAGE

You are a South Carolinian. South Carolina is your home. It is a part of your heritage.

Earlier South Carolinians have passed on to you a rich history. They have passed on a beautiful environment. You can help pass these on to new South Carolinians.

This chapter is about how South Carolinians are preserving our heritage. You will learn things you can do to help.

Finding The Past

Think back over what you have learned about our past. Think about the people who once lived where you live now.

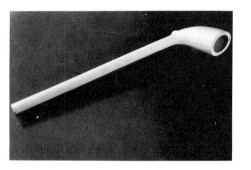

We have written records about some parts of our past. But there are no written records about other parts. How can we know about things that were not written down?

Scientists called **archaeologists** study the past. They can learn about the past without written records. They look for **evidence,** or clues, about earlier people.

Archaeologists want to know about early South Carolina. They ask questions. For example, What did early South Carolinians eat and wear? How did they work and play? Then they look for evidence to help them answer the questions.

Often they look for places where earlier settlers might have lived. These places are called **sites.** There are sites of early South Carolinians throughout our state. Some are even under water! These sites help us know about our past.

At each site archaeologists look for **artifacts.** These are objects left by people of the past. Archaeologists also look for pieces of old buildings. Artifacts and ruins of old buildings are evidence of our past. They tell us how earlier South Carolinians lived.

Archaeologists at USC find and preserve evidence of our past. They keep records of all known sites. They study each new site that is found. And they keep maps of each site. They label, bag, and box artifacts found in fields, forests, and even under water. They also have a small museum in Columbia. There they display artifacts thousands of years old.

Sometimes sites are destroyed. When we build new homes, roads, shopping malls, and lakes, we may ruin important sites.

Laws now protect important sites. These laws let archaeologists study an area before people start building there. Still, hundreds of sites in South Carolina are being destroyed by roads, dams, homes, and industry.

Some sites are destroyed when people dig things up without thinking. All of us need to know what to do if we find an artifact or discover an important site. Then we could do a better job of protecting our heritage.

A Dig

Would you know what to do if you found an artifact? Listen to the story.

Keowee dam site, 1967

READ TO ME

Imagine that you and your friends are walking through the woods. Suddenly, you trip. As your friends help you up, they see some interesting stone tools caked with mud. They also see part of what looks like an **ancient,** or very old, clay pot. Where did these come from? How long have they been here?

You report what you find to an archaeologist. The archaeologist thinks that your find may be an important discovery. A team of scientists comes to your site to study, mark, and map the area. A **botanist** studies the plants in the area. She tries to identify the seeds and nuts found near the old clay pot. A **geologist** studies the tools. He knows a lot about rocks. He tries to identify the kinds of rocks used to make the tools. A **zoologist** studies bones in the area to find out what animals they came from.

Your discovery turns out to be really important. More archaeologists arrive every day. Some dig very carefully to find more things of value. They even sift the soil for very small artifacts. Many of these are tagged and kept for more study.

The archaeologists are studying your site by digging into the soil. They call your site a **dig.** Studying a dig takes hard work and patience.

The archaeologists make careful notes and draw special maps. They want to remember each artifact and where they found it. They take many pictures, too.

Your site is so important that archaeologists decide to rebuild it. Photographers get into planes and fly over your dig to take pictures from the air. With maps, artifacts, and pictures, archaeologists begin to make a model of what your site actually was like thousands of years ago. This is a special way to preserve our past.

Who was most important in this preservation project? **You** were! You did not destroy the site, and you reported it to an archaeologist. You made it possible for the dig to begin. How does it feel to be so important?

Historic Preservation

Some South Carolinians save buildings and places important in our more recent history. These people are interested in **historic preservation.** They save and restore old houses. They study unusual buildings in our state. And they save objects used by South Carolinians in earlier times. Some places are important to our state as well as to our community. Often these are places where state leaders lived. They may be places where important things happened.

Mulberry Plantation

Rose Hill

Rose Hill in Union County was a cotton plantation. It was the home of William Gist. He was once Governor of South Carolina.

In those days most governors lived in their own homes instead of in Columbia. Much state business was done at Governor Gist's home at Rose Hill.

You can visit Rose Hill today. It has been restored. South Carolina has helped to save it by making it a state park.

Old St. David's Church, Cheraw

The United States has a list of many places important in our country's history. It is called the **National Register of Historic Places.** It is an honor for a place to be listed in the Register.

Many South Carolina buildings are listed in the Register. Among these are houses, churches, office buildings, lighthouses, and forts.

Some whole areas of South Carolina are important parts of our history. These areas are called **historic districts.** The Register lists many historic districts in our state.

Buildings and objects from the past remind us of who we are. They remind us of our ancestors. They remind us of what it means to be a South Carolinian.

Conservation

Many South Carolinians work to save, or **conserve,** our natural environment. Some work for our South Carolina government. They help farmers and other people use soil wisely. They make sure that mines, dams, and reservoirs are run well. They look after our beaches, dunes, coastal wetlands, and coastal waters. And they work to prevent forest fires.

One part of our government is the Department of Wildlife and Marine (sea) Resources. It protects endangered plants and animals.

DO YOU KNOW?

The Department of Wildlife and Marine Resources prints a magazine. It is called *South Carolina Wildlife.*

Have you used this magazine in your class? It can help you learn about our South Carolina environment. Read it to find out about our environment and how to protect it.

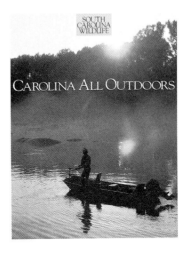

Our government has set aside areas as state parks and state forests. It protects the plants and animals in these areas.

It has also set up the Heritage Trust Program. The Heritage Trust provides money to buy and protect natural land areas in our state.

Our U.S. government helps with conservation, too. Do you remember any of our national wildlife refuges? Do you live near any of our national forests?

Many South Carolinians are interested in conserving the environment. Sometimes they work together in groups. Have you heard of the Audubon Society or the Sierra Club? How about the Wildlife Federation or the Garden Club of South Carolina? You may join one of these groups some day to help conserve our environment.

Even now you can help keep our environment beautiful. You can pick up trash. You can help keep our rivers and streams clean. These are things every citizen can do. Can you think of others?

Because you live in South Carolina, part of your heritage comes from this state. South Carolina has a long, rich past. Citizens have worked hard to help us remember our state history.

South Carolina also has a beautiful environment. Many South Carolinians are helping to conserve it.

South Carolina is your home. How can you preserve your heritage for your children and their children?

The South Carolina Museum in Columbia is a special place. It is in an old mill on the Congaree River. You can see marks on the floors where the old textile machines used to be.

Our state museum is a good place to learn about South Carolina. You can learn about both our natural environment and our history.

If you visit the museum, you will see a real-size model of the *Best Friend of Charleston.* You will see an old schoolroom and an old store. What other things from our history would you put in the museum? What things about our environment would you want to show?

A CLOSER LOOK
A STATE MUSEUM

Artists help preserve our heritage. They do this by painting and drawing people and scenes they see in our state.

Some artists paint **portraits** of people. We know what early South Carolinians looked like because of portraits.

We also know about wildlife in the early days because of artists. One of our early wildlife painters was Maria Martin from Charleston.

Many scenes of life in our state have been preserved by artists like Elizabeth O'Neill Verner from Charleston. Some of these works are in art **galleries,** homes, and public buildings.

A CLOSER LOOK
ARTISTS

In the Bend of Church Street   etching by Elizabeth O'Neill Verner

UNIT 6 REVIEW

Reviewing Main Ideas

1. Who are you? Use everything you have learned to explain your answer.
2. What kinds of things do families do to preserve their heitage?
3. How are South Carolinians different from each other? How have these differences been good for our state?
4. What can communities do to preserve our heritage?
5. Why is it important to conserve the environment?

Using New Vocabulary

Think about the new words below. Arrange them in two or three groups to that each word fits in only one group. Name the groups. Be ready to explain your work.

customs	council	mayor	site
town hall	archaeologist	museum	artifact
generation	reunion	dig	ancestor

Can you think of another way to group these words?

Remembering People and Places

Make your own halls of fame for South Carolina. Make one for people and the other for places. Pick the first five people and places to go in your halls of fame. Explain why you chose each one.

Thinking About South Carolina

1. Which of these people would you prefer to be: historian, geographer, archaeologist? Why?
2. Suppose your school wanted to preserve its heritage. Make a plan to show your school a way to do this.
3. Find a place in your community or neighborhood you think should be preserved. Explain your choice.
4. A time capsule is a box of artifacts. Suppose you are making a time capsule to tell about this year in your life. What artifacts would you include? Why?

Being Creative

Travel companies often use posters to show what is special about places. Make a travel poster which invites people to visit or live in South Carolina. Be sure it shows what is special about our state.

CONCLUSION

This book has been about you. You are a South Carolinian. That means you live in a beautiful state. Your state stretches from the beaches of the Low Country to the mountains of the Up Country. It has high lands and low lands, wet lands and dry lands. It has many rare and beautiful plants and animals.

Your state has many resources for people to use. South Carolinians have used these resources to make a living. They have used them to make our state a good place to live. These resources are important to our state. South Carolinians work hard to protect them.

Your state has a history. It was home for the First South Carolinians. It was home for settlers from other parts of the world. Your state helped to form our country, the United States.

South Carolina has changed since then. Many people helped our state grow and change. They have passed on to us reminders of how our state grew. They have left a valuable heritage.

In many ways South Carolinians are different from each other. We are men, women, girls, or boys. We are white, black, red, or yellow. We are young or old. Some of us have lived in South Carolina a long time. Others have lived here a short time. Each of us has different customs.

But we learn from each other, and we learn

215

about each other. We remember ways we are alike. We work side by side. We have the same leaders. Together we have a rich heritage.

Because you are a South Carolinian, this heritage belongs to you. How will you care for it? How will you pass it on?

Glossary

academy (n.), a school somewhat like our high school. Parents paid to have their children go there.

advice (n.), information or ideas about what to do

advisor (n.), someone who gives advice

agriculture (n.), farming

album (n.), a book with blank pages where photographs can be kept

algae (n.), tiny green plants that can cling to rocks in swift streams

American Revolution (n.), war fought by American colonists to become independent from England

ancestors (n.), earlier family members

ancient (adj.), very old; from times long past

anniversary (n.), the same date in a later year

archaeologist (n.), a scientist who studies evidence of human life in past times

architect (n.), a person who plans or designs buildings

artifact (n.), an object left by people of the past

astronaut (n.), someone who goes into space to explore

auction (n.), a special sale where buyers bid for items. The highest bid gets the item.

auctioneer (n.), a person who runs an auction

barbecue (n.), meat roasted over an open fire, today served with a special sauce

barrens (n.), areas of land where few plants grow

barrier island (n.), an island which protects the coast from ocean winds and surf

battle (n.), fighting between two groups of soldiers

bay (n.), a large arm of the ocean which stretches into the land

beach (n.), a stretch of sand along the edge of an ocean

beach music (n.), a kind of music popular in the 1960s

bid (v.), to offer to pay a certain price; (n.), an offer to pay a certain price

blockade (n.), the closing of a harbor to enemy ships

bluffs (n.), high, steep cliffs or river banks

boll (n.), the cluster in which cotton grows on the cotton plant

boll weevil (n.), an insect that destroys cotton bolls

botanist (n.), a scientist who studies plants

boundary (n.), a line which marks the edges of a piece of land, a town, a country, etc.

British (adj.), English; from the island of Great Britain

business (n.), a store, factory, or shop which buys and sells goods and/or services

canal (n.), a human-made waterway

canebrake (n.), an area by a stream which is covered with tall cane

cannon (n.), a large gun which fires iron balls

canoe (n.), a light boat with pointed ends, moved by paddles or oars

capital (n.), a city where the government of a country or state is located

cargo (n.), goods carried by a ship, plane, or truck

Carolina bay (n.), a large, oval area of land that looks as if a giant fist had slammed into the earth

cemetery (n.), a graveyard

ceremony (n.), a special event in which people follow customs, such as a wedding

chapel (n.), a place of worship in a school

217

chief (n.), the leader or top person

citizen (n.), a person who lives in a town or city

city hall (n.), a building where a city government meets

Civil War (n.), the war in the United States between the North and the South

claimed (v.), said one owned or had a right to something

clan (n.), a large family group which is a part of a tribe

climate (n.), usual type of weather in an area over a long period of time

clog (n.), a dance done in heavy shoes with heavy, stamping steps

coast (n.), the area of land next to the ocean

coastal plain (n.), an area of flat land between the coast and the Midlands

cobblestone (n.), a large, rounded stone used to weigh down an empty ship, then used to pave streets in coastal cities

college (n.), a kind of school which comes after high school

colonist (n.), a person who lives in a colony

colony (n.), a settlement or group of settlements far away from the home country

community (n.), a group of people who live and work together in an area; a neighborhood, a town, or a city

Confederate States of America (n.), the new country set up by the South during the Civil War

Congress (n.), the part of the U.S. government that makes the laws

conserve (v.), to save something so it will not be lost or used up

Constitution of the United States (n.), the written paper which set up the government of the United States

container ship (n.), a ship which carries containers full of goods

continent (n.), one of the seven large land areas on the earth

cotton gin (n.), a machine which removes seeds from cotton

council (n.), a group of representatives that makes decisions for a larger group or community

country (n.), the land and people under a government which is not under any other government

county (n.), an area of a state which has its own government to take care of needs of people in that area

county seat (n.), town or city where county government buildings are located

cowcatcher (n.), an iron piece in front of a railroad engine which helps clear the track

cowpens (n.), fenced areas where cattle are kept

cradle board (n.), a board to which Indians tied their babies to flatten the babies' heads

craft (n.), a skill in making something by hand

crane (n.), a machine which lifts and moves large, heavy objects

crank (n.), a handle which is turned to start or run a machine

creative (adj.), able to find new and better ways to do things

credit (n.), trust that a buyer will pay at a future time. A buyer pays interest for credit.

crop (n.), a plant grown for food or for sale

crossroads (n.), a place where two roads meet

culture (n.), how people live—the kinds of work they do, the tools they use, what they eat, how they dress, etc.

cure (v.), to preserve or save by drying

customs (n.), ways of doing things passed from one generation to another

dairy products (n.), items such as milk, cheese, and butter

dam (n.), a wall built across a river or stream

deciduous (adj.), losing leaves in the fall

Declaration of Independence (n.), the written paper in which the colonies said they were free from the English government

depot (n.), a station on a railroad line

diary (n.), a daily record of a person's experiences and thoughts; the book in which this record is written

dig (n.), a place where archaeologists are digging for artifacts

directions (n.), words which tell which way to go to get from one place to another

dock (v.), to steer a boat to a dock or platform on the shore

drawbridge (n.), a bridge that can be raised or moved aside to allow boats to pass underneath

drought (n.), a dry time when little rain falls and the land and plants begin to dry up

dugout (n.), a log canoe

dunes (n.), high piles of sand on the beach

Earth (n.), the planet on which we live

east (n.), one of the main, or cardinal, directions; (adj. or adv.), in or toward the east

ebb (v.), to go out or fall away from the land

educator (n.), a teacher

elected (v.), chose for office by voting

endangered (adj.), in danger of dying out or disappearing from the earth

erode (v.), to wear away, as in erosion

erosion (n.), the wearing away of land by water, wind, and sun

evergreen (n.), a tree which stays green all year long

evidence (n.), a clue

experiment (v.), to try things to see what works and what does not work

explorer (n.), a person who travels to an unknown area to see what is there

factory (n.), a building where people make goods such as cloth, shoes, cars, etc.

fad (n.), something that is popular for only a short time

fair (n.), an event where farm goods are shown and there are rides and other activities for fun

fall line (n.), the belt of land where the high land of the Piedmont drops to the low land of the coastal plain

family tree (n.), a drawing or diagram that shows family members, how they are related, and when they lived

ferry (n.), a boat which carries people, goods, wagons, cars, etc. across a body of water

fertile (adj.), rich with minerals so plants can grow

fertilizer (n.), something put into the soil to make it rich enough for plants to grow

festival (n.), a special celebration

fiber (n.), a strand of a material like cotton or wool which can be spun into yarn

floodplain (n.), a low, flat area beside a river or stream that is sometimes flooded by river or stream water

food chain (n.), a series of plants and animals, each of which is food for another

forestry (n.), the science of taking care of forests and trees

fossils (n.), remains of plants and animals which lived thousands of years ago

freighter (n.), a ship which carries goods

freshwater marsh (n.), marsh in which the water comes from a river, stream, or lake or from rain

gallery (n.), a special room or building where paintings are shown

General Assembly (n.), group of representatives who make laws for South Carolina

generation (n.), a time in family history

generator (n.), a machine that turns water power into electricity

geography (n.), the study of places

geologist (n.), a scientist who studies rocks

globe (n.), a model of the earth

gourd (n.), a hard-shelled vegetable which can be used as a musical instrument or made into a tool

government (n.), an organization which rules a group of people

governor (n.), a title given to the head of the government of a colony or a state

grain (n.), the small, hard seed of plants like wheat, barley, and rice

granite (n.), a very hard rock used for buildings and monuments

great circles (n.), the lines which make up the grid on a globe

grid (n.), a pattern of evenly spaced lines which helps to locate points on a map

grist mill (n.), a factory where grain is ground into meal or flour

grits (n.), a vegetable dish made by grinding corn kernels

Gullah (n.), a special language in South Carolina. It comes from African and colonial English.

habitat (n.), natural environment which provides a home for wildlife

hammock (n.), a piece of netting hung between two trees and used as a bed

harbor (n.), an area where large ships can come in to land

harbor pilot (n.), someone who guides ships in and out of a harbor

harvest (v.), to cut or pick a crop when it is ready

hatchery (n.), a place where fish are raised from eggs

headquarters (n.), a place where military officers meet to make decisions

heritage (n.), ideas, traditions, and things passed on by those who have lived before us

hero (n.), a person who performs an act of courage or makes an important contribution

historian (n.), a person who studies the past

historic district (n.), an area which is an important part of our history

historic preservation (n.), the act of keeping places important to our past safe from harm or change

history (n.), the study of things that have happened

hominy (n.), puffed corn kernels

hospital (n.), a place where people take care of others who are sick or hurt

House of Representatives (n.), a group of lawmakers; one part of the U.S. Congress and the S.C. General Assembly

Huguenot (n.), a French settler who came to the New World in order to worship in his/her own way

human resources (n.), people

hurricane (n.), a big storm with heavy rain and high winds

hydroelectric power (n.), electricity made by the power of water going over a dam

independent (adj.), free to rule oneself

index (n.), an alphabetical list of terms, usually found in the back of a book or atlas

Indians (n.), name given by Columbus to Native Americans

indigo (n.), a plant that makes a blue dye

industry (n.), a group of companies that produce and sell a certain type of good or service

inlet (n.), an arm of the sea which reaches into the land

inn (n.), a hotel

invent (v.), to create, to make something new

inventory (n.), a list of the items or supplies in a given area, such as a house or a store

irrigation (n.), a way of watering fields during dry times or droughts

island (n.), a piece of land with water on all sides

jazz (n.), a form of lively music begun in the South

judge (n.), one who settles arguments, often in a court of law

junction (n.), a place where two lines of railroad track meet

kaolin (n.), a special clay used for fine pottery and other products

kernel (n.), the inner, softer part of a seed

kudzu (n.), a vine used to control erosion

law (n.), a rule for a state or a country

league (n.), a group of teams that play one another

legend (n.), a story retold through the years by many different people. Parts of the story may have been changed in the retelling.

located (v.), placed or found

location (n.), place where something can be found

Lords Proprietors (n.), English noblemen who first owned the Carolinas

Low Country (n.), area between the Atlantic Ocean and the middle of the state; made up of the coast and the coastal plain

lumber (n.), boards cut from trees

maize (n.), Indian corn

mammals (n.), animals which have hair or fur

mansion (n.), a fine, large house

map (n.), a flat picture or drawing of the earth or a part of the earth

mariculture (n.), the raising of sea animals in special pools of sea water

marsh (n.), grassland covered with water

mayor (n.), leader or chief officer of a town or city government

meal (n.), a coarse flour such as corn meal

Midlands (n.), area in the middle of the state which stretches from Aiken County, through Columbia, to Chesterfield County

military academy (n.), a school for young men who plan to become soldiers

mill (n.), a factory

minerals (n.), materials like stone, coal, salt, or oil, which are taken from the ground for people's use

missionaries (n.), people who travel to other lands to spread their religious beliefs

money crop (n.), a plant grown for sale

museum (n.), a building used to store and display items from our history

national monument (n.), an area saved and protected by the U.S. government. The Congaree Swamp is a national monument.

National Register (n.), a list of places important in the history of the United States

Native Americans (n.), people who lived here before settlers came from other countries; sometimes called Indians

natural environment (n.), the land and all the living things on the land

natural resource (n.), a resource which comes from the natural environment

New World (n.), name given to the Americas when they were first discovered by Europeans

north (n.), one of the main, or cardinal, directions; (adj. or adv.), in or toward the north

North America (n.), name of the continent we live on

northeast (n.), one of the in-between, or intermediate, directions; (adj. or adv.), between north and east

Glossary   221

northwest (n.), one of the in-between, or intermediate, directions; (adj. or adv.), between north and west

obey (v.), to follow, to do what one is told

ocean (n.), a huge body of salt water

officer (n.), leader of a group of soldiers, such as a colonel or a general; an elected leader of a government, such as a president or a governor

orchard (n.), a field planted with fruit trees

ore (n.), a mineral mixed with dirt and rock

palisade (n.), a wall around a town, usually made of logs

pasture (n.), a grassy field where cattle graze

Patriot (n.), name for a colonist who fought for independence from England

paved (adj.), covered with a hard surface to make travel easier

peace treaty (n.), an agreement not to fight

permanent (adj.), lasting

photograph (n.), a picture taken with a camera

Piedmont (n.), part of the Up Country. Its name means the land "at the foot" or bottom of the mountains.

pirate (n.), someone who attacks and robs ships

pitchfork (n.), a tool the size of a shovel which looks like a large fork and is used to lift hay

placer gold (n.), gold found in sand and gravel in a streambed

plantation (n.), a large farm where money crops were grown. Many had slaves to do the work in the fields.

planter (n.), owner of a plantation

population (n.), number of people

port (n.), a city or town which has a harbor used for trade

portrait (n.), a painting of a person

pottery (n.), items like bowls and dishes which are made of clay

poultry (n.), chickens, turkeys, ducks, and geese; birds raised for food

preserve (v.), to save

President (n.), leader or chief elected officer of the U.S. who carries out the laws

quarry (n.), an open pit from which rock is mined

quill pen (n.), a writing tool made from a feather, usually a goose feather

quilt (n.), a bed covering which has a design made of pieces of cloth

rapids (n.), places in a river or stream where the water splashes and swirls over rocks

Rebel (n.), name given to Patriots in the American Revolution and to Confederate soldiers in the Civil War

recent (adj.), happened just a little while ago

recipe (n.), a set of directions for making a certain kind of food

records (n.), written information that people keep so they will remember it

recreation (n.), fun

refuge (n.), a safe place for wild animals and plants where they are protected from people

relatives (n.), people who are members of the same family

religious freedom (n.), right to worship as one wants; right to go to the church one chooses

represent (v.), to stand for or act for

representative (n.), person selected by others to stand for or act for them in a council or law-making group; a member of the House of Representatives

reservation (n.), land set aside especially for a group of Indians

reservoir (n.), a large pool or lake for storing water

resort (n.), a place people go for vacation

resource (n.), something people use to help them make and do other things

reunion (n.), a gathering of members of a group, such as a family, that has been separated

river (n.), a long stream of flowing water

river system (n.), a network of rivers and the smaller streams that run into them

royal colony (n.), a colony under the rule of the King of England

royal governor (n.), the person a king or queen made head of the government of a colony

rural (adj.), away from the city, in farming areas

salt marsh (n.), marsh which is flooded by salty ocean water

Sand Hills (n.), rolling hills of sandy soil found in the Midlands

sandbar (n.), a bar of sand formed in a stream by bits of soil carried by the water from higher levels

sawmill (n.), a factory where trees are cut into boards or lumber

scholarship (n.), a money award which helps a student pay for education

scout (n.), a person sent out to gather information about the land or enemy ahead

scrapbook (n.), a large book with blank pages on which photographs, pictures, and newspaper stories can be pasted

seceded (v.), said it was no longer a member or part of something

Senate (n.), a group of lawmakers; one part of the Congress and the General Assembly

Senator (n.), member of the Senate; one kind of representative in the Congress and the General Assembly

services (n.), things people do for other people

settlement (n.), a new town; a community of settlers

settlers (n.), people from many European countries who came to early South Carolina to live

sharecropper (n.), a farmer who farmed someone else's land and gave part of his crop to the landowner

shoals (n.), shallow areas in a river or stream where water flows over and around sandbars

site (n.), a piece of land where something is or was located

slate (n.), a smooth, rock-like surface on which one can write with chalk

slaves (n.), people taken from their homes and made to work for someone else. Slaves are not free to do what they want.

soldiers (n.), fighting men; members of an army

sound (n.), a calm body of water which lies between a barrier island and the coast

south (n.), one of the main, or cardinal, directions; (adj. or adv.), in or toward the south

southeast (n.), one of the in-between, or intermediate, directions; (adj. or adv.), between south and east

southwest (n.), one of the in-between, or intermediate, directions; (adj. or adv.), between south and west

South Carolina (n.), a state of the United States, next to Georgia, North Carolina, and the Atlantic Ocean

South Carolinian (n.), a person who lives in South Carolina; a person who was born in South Carolina

soybeans (n.), a plant grown because it is good food for cattle, its seed makes good food for people, and it improves the soil

specialize (v.), to do one particular kind of work

Glossary   223

stagecoach (n.), a carriage which took paying passengers

state (n.), an area of a larger country which has its own government. South Carolina is a state of the United States of America.

state house (n.), the building in which the state legislature meets

statue (n.), a likeness of someone or something, made of stone, metal, or wood

steam engine (n.), a machine that runs with steam power

steeplechase (n.), a horse race across grassy fields

storyteller (n.), a person who tells or writes stories

submarine (n.), a ship that travels underwater

suburban (adj.), right outside a city

suburbs (n.), communities right outside a city

succulent (n.), a kind of plant which is able to store water in its leaves so that it can survive in a dry area

supplies (n.), necessary materials

Supreme Court (n.), the name of the highest court in a state or country

surf (n.), white-capped waves of the ocean

surrender (v.), to give up in defeat

swamp (n.), a flooded forest; a low, forested area which is covered with water

taproot (n.), a long, thick root which reaches deep into the soil to find water

taxes (n.), money which is paid to the government

terminal (n.), a large area where ships, trains, trucks, or planes begin and end trips

textiles (n.), yarn, thread, cloth, and goods made from cloth

tidal marsh (n.), a salt marsh; a marsh which is flooded by ocean tides

tide (n.), movement of ocean water

tobacco (n.), a plant which has large leaves used for smoking

toll (n.), a charge made to cross a river by bridge or boat or to travel on certain roads

tombstone (n.), a gravestone

Tories (n.), a name given to colonists who remained loyal to England during the American Revolution

tornado (n.), a wind storm which looks like a long, narrow cloud. The cloud is made of strong, whirling winds which can cause damage.

tourist (n.), a traveler; someone who is traveling for fun or recreation

town hall (n.), a building where the town government meets

tribe (n.), an organization of groups of people who have the same ancestors, language, customs, and beliefs

truck farmer (n.), one who raises fruits and vegetables, usually on a small farm, and uses a truck to take the crop to market

tutor (n.), a teacher paid by parents to teach the children in a family

Union (n.), the name given to the Northern states during the Civil War

United States of America (n.), the country in which we live

university (n.), a school which continues education beyond high school

Up Country (n.), area which stretches from the middle of South Carolina to the northwest corner, made up of the mountains and the Piedmont

urban (adj.), having to do with a city or city life

valley (n.), a large, low area between areas of high land varieties (n.), kinds

vermiculite (n.), a mineral that easily takes in water and is used in potting plants

victory (n.), a win, as in a game or a war

village (n.), a group of homes; a very small town

waterfall (n.), area where water falls from the upper part of a stream to the lower part of the stream

waterwheel (n.), a large wheel turned by a stream to provide power to a mill

weather (n.), the condition of the air at a particular time. For example, it can be rainy or sunny, hot or cold.

west (n.), one of the main, or cardinal, directions; (adj. or adv.), in or toward the west

wetlands (n.), low areas covered by water all or part of the time

White House (n.), home of the President of the United States in Washington, D.C.

wildlife (n.), animals and plants that are growing on their own in nature

Yankees (n.), a name used for Union soldiers

Index

Acknowledgments

We gratefully acknowledge the assistance of many individuals and organizations whose contributions were crucial in the making of this text. We found friendly cooperation from state agencies and offices. Howard Preston, Robert Powell, and Jane Proctor provided helpful comments on the text as it was in process. We are especially thankful to the principals, third-grade teachers, and students at Cannons, Clifdale, and Jonesville Elementary Schools, where pilot testing was conducted. Their valuable suggestions contributed greatly to the final copy of this book. We would like to express our appreciation to the many teachers and students involved in *Sandlapper's Corner* through the years for their enthusiasm for learning about their state. Their interest, and that of so many of our friends in public education, pointed out the need for such a book. For photographs we are indebted to Mark Olencki, Sandra Powell, Frazer Pajak, Kathy Bell, Don Hendrix, and Jerry Howe. We are grateful to Constance Schulz for allowing us to use slides from *The History of South Carolina Slide Collection,* a fine resource of slides for teachers, published by Sandlapper Publishing Company and Instructional Resources Corporation. We appreciate the professional assistance of publisher Frank Handal, designer Faith Nance, and sales representative Bob Bell. Producing a text is a team effort, and we are glad they have been on our team. Finally, we would like to thank our friends and colleagues for their encouragement and support and our families for their love and patience during the five years this book has been in production. A special thank you is in order for Howard Thomas for doing double duty with family responsibilities, freeing his wife to write.

Credits

Key: Left (l), Right (r), Top (t), Bottom (b)

Art Carter,   23 (bl and br), 37 (tl), 150 (t)
  Color 2-p. 4 (t)

The Charleston Museum, 119

Robert Clark,   27 (4th from left)

Clemson University,   129 (b), 130 (bl, br).

Coker's Pedigreed Seed Company,   165

College of Charleston,   109 (l)

Columbia Chamber of Commerce,   179 (m)

William A. Conklin,   23 (t)

Cornell University Libraries, Department of
  Manuscripts & University Archives, 111 (br)

Greater Cheraw Chamber of Commerce,   208 (b)
  102, 127

Mike Creel,   Color 2-p. 3 (b)

Duke Power Company,   148 (t), 214 (tl)

Darby Erd,   Illustrations 58, 59, 60, 63, 64 (b), 65,
  66, 67, 71, 80, 81, 152, 153

Ernest Ferguson,   149 (t), 169 (t)

Florence Morning News,   193

Charles Gay,   76, 77, 110 (tl), 116, 117 (tr), 118, 122

The Herald (Rock Hill, S.C.),   69 (l), 146 (b),
  198 (t), 201 (ml, mr)

The History of South Carolina Slide Collection
  (c. Constance Schulz),   22 (t), 86, 119 (b),
  120 (b), 127 (b) 131, 132 (t), 135, 136, 160, 162 (r),
  171 (b), 176, 195 (b) Back cover (b), Front
  cover (t, m, br), Color 1-p.3 (tl), p.4 (t, l),
  Color 2-p.2 (br),

Phillip Jones,   174 (b)

Library of Congress,   115, 117 (tl)

Magnolia Plantation & Gardens,   198 (b)

McKissick Museum (USC),   204

Middleton Place,   87

Museum of the Cherokee Indian,   69 (b)

National Gallery of Art,   96 (t)

Mark Olenki,   vii (m and b), vii (2nd from top),
  33 (t), 39, 42, 94, 130 (t), 157, 166 (t), 179 (l), 185
  (t), 197 (tl and tr), 203

Orangeburg County Library,   186

Frazer Pajak,   vii (tl), 11 (r), 147 (br)

Pennsylvania Academy of the Fine Arts,   104 (tl)

Phil Powell,   Color 2-p. 2 (t, r)

Courtland Richards,   Color 2-p. 1 (bl, br)

Robin Richards,   Cover-map, illustrations 50, 78,
  83, 108

Schlesinger Library, Radcliffe College,   111 (bl)

Bill Scoggins,   110 (tr)

S.C. Department of Agriculture,   107 (t), 158

S.C. Department of Archives and History,   97 (t),
  125 (t), 168 (b)

S.C. Department of Parks, Recreation and
  Tourism,   22 (b), 209 (t)

S.C. Historical Society,   117 (b)

S.C. Institute for Archaeology,   205

S.C. Ports Authority,   144, 145

S.C. State House Collection,   96 (m, b)

S.C. State Museum,   211 (t, m)

S.C. Textile Manufacturers Association,
  166 (br, bl)

SCDWMR,   20 (b), 23 (bm), 27 (2nd, 3rd, 5th from
  left), 28 (b), 36, 38 (top, 2nd from top), 41 (t), 47,
  (t), 48 (t), 50 (l), 51, 53 (t, m), 209 (b) Back cover
  (t), Color 1-p. 3 (tr), 2-p. 1 (tr), p. 2 (l), p. 4 (b),

South Caroliniana Library,   x, viii (b)

The State (Columbia, S.C.),   172 (b)

Bryan Stone,   maps throughout book

Richard Taylor,   77 (t), 161

University of South Carolina,   109 (r)

U.S. Fish & Wildlife Service,   41 (2nd from top)

Tom Vargo,   24 (t), 25 (m), 26 (bl, br), 28 (t),
  29 (m), 43, 174 (t) Back Cover (l), Color 1-p. 1

Elizabeth O'Neill Verner Studio-Musem,
  211 (b)

Cecil J. Williams,   29 (t), 46, 69 (r), 110 (b), 132 (b),
  134, 140 (l), 143, 151, 164 (b), 172 (tl, tr), 192 (b),
  194 (t,m), 196 (l), 207, 208 (t), 214 (br), 215 (m),
  216 (bl) Color 1-p. 4 (t)

York County Historical Commission   201 (ml, mr)